THE RISE AND FALL OF STATES

ACCORDING TO GREEK AUTHORS

JEROME LECTURES   ELEVENTH SERIES

The Rise and Fall of States According to Greek Authors

Jacqueline de Romilly

ANN ARBOR   THE UNIVERSITY OF MICHIGAN PRESS

Acknowledgments

This book consists of the four Jerome Lectures which I had the honor of delivering at the University of Michigan in September, 1973, and at the American Academy in Rome the following year.

I should like, therefore, to express my gratitude, not only to the generous founder of the Jerome Lectures, but also to the various colleagues whose hospitality made these occasions both enjoyable and stimulating—especially my old friend Gerry Else. It would also be unfair not to say how thankful I am to the University of Michigan Press: it needed real patience to deal with a manuscript prepared for lecturing and written by a foreigner. Whatever may still be incorrect in the presentation of the book is certainly nobody's fault but mine.

Contents

I

The Pattern of History

My theme is not a modest one. Even restricted to the main Greek historians who dealt with the rise and fall of states, from Herodotus to Polybius, it is wide and ambitious (although from time to time it may be worthwhile to try to see the whole picture). Yet, I shall start with something even more general, for a correct interpretation of the Greek ideas about the rise and fall of states can only be reached if we first know whether or not these ideas were related to a general view of the pattern of history as a whole. It is my opinion that they were not. But some misunderstanding can arise, for the moderns have often developed such general views by using hints and suggestions that did exist in Greek authors, hence the easy temptation of ascribing to them the theory itself. Tracing the origin and birth of these theories will therefore be necessary if we want to understand how much more reasonable the Greeks were in this matter than we often believe them to have been—or indeed than we are nowadays.

I shall show this by a survey of the evidence, proving, first, they had no idea of a continuous progress in history and, second, they had no idea of a general rule or rhythm that would have commanded the rise and fall of all states, whatever their conditions or policy.

That the Greeks had no idea of a continuous trend in history applies both to pessimistic and to optimistic patterns. What I call a pessimistic pattern involves the notion that history shows a perpetual degradation of things, changing always for the worse, in a more or less regular manner. This is, no doubt, a Greek idea. Two authors, Hesiod and Plato, afford some support to those who believe that it governed the Greek view of history. Yet, even for these two authors, matters are not as clearcut as they would seem to be.

Hesiod's view appears in the myth about the five successive ages (*Works and Days* 109–202). As everybody knows, these ages are the Golden Age, the Silver Age, the Bronze Age, the Heroic Age, and the Iron Age, which includes the present era. But two remarks should be made from the start. The first is that, even in this field, which is the free field of myth and imagination, Hesiod's mind didn't succeed in keeping to the pessimistic trend of his non-Greek sources: the Heroic Age, which destroys the coherent system of metals, has a population more just and more brave than the preceding one.[1] The second remark is that all human history belongs to the Iron Age. The beings who precede the Iron Age are, in fact, very different from mankind, and live in very different conditions (for instance, they don't get old, they don't have to grow plants for their food, they die after having been children for a hundred years, they are born from trees, and so on). History is therefore outside the pattern of degenerescence.

This would also apply to Plato's myth in the *Politicus* but would not apply to his analysis of constitutions in Book VIII of the *Republic* or in Book III of the *Laws* where he does deal with historical time. But, even supposing his pattern of evolution to be a chronological and historical description, which is obviously difficult to admit, he still doesn't deal with states and still less with their power. In the *Republic*, he judges constitutions according to moral standards and would certainly not consider the rise of a city as a sign of good health and sanity. Only in the *Laws* does he show the shortcomings of several states and constitutions bringing on their collapse, but then he doesn't try to find between these separate downfalls any regular succession toward the worse. He has three main states, corresponding to three different lessons, each equal to the other, and he obviously wishes this threefold lesson to help foster a move toward the better—as he also did in the *Republic*.

No doubt such texts may suggest a pessimistic tone or view. They are, however, far from decisive either in content or in number.[2] In fact there has always been, in Greece as in every civilization, a sort of everlasting dispute between those who were moralists, living in the regret of the so-called Golden Age, and those who were realists, admiring the results of civilization as such and enjoying both prosperity and political success.[3] But on the whole, if we leave aside the two authors just mentioned, who didn't really feel themselves members of the city-state—one because it hadn't yet grown up to maturity, the other because he shrank from it through disappointment— it is clear that the most natural tendency of Greek authors, and particularly of Greek historians, was to insist as much as possible on what I have called the optimistic pattern.

The greatest of Greek historians, Herodotus and Thucydides, both wrote histories of a large power that had just been defeated or destroyed. Herodotus wrote about the war which produced the Persian disaster in Greece; Thucydides wrote about the war in which Athens's power was ruined. Yet, neither of them wrote a work that could be called "Decline and Fall." Herodotus's work begins with five books (more than half the work), which deal with the growth, or rise, of Persia. Even after her defeat, no conclusion seems to emerge in regard to its reasons or consequences. Thucydides also dwells on the growth of Athens—he does so not only in the long digression about the formation of the empire (I. 89-118), but in each of his speeches, and all these speeches, whether Athenian or not, insist on the idea that this growth is almost irresistible. Certainly one can read in Herodotus and in Thucydides an analysis of the causes leading to ruin. We shall try to trace them in the following chapters. But the emphasis, the interest, the wonder seem to be centered on the growth at least as much as on the fall.

Indeed, of all Greek authors, Thucydides came closest to the idea of a regular progress of power in human development. In the first chapters of Book I, he describes the growth of power, from one state to another, each one in turn getting larger and wider. Athens is at the end of this evolution. There is no doubt that Athens fell, but the general trend of thought that runs through these pages could almost suggest the idea that after Athens, later and elsewhere, another power could rise and become still greater. Thucydides does not say it or suggest it in any manner, but a reader, being less engaged in contemporary circumstances, could form such an idea after having read his work.

Indeed, some centuries later this power rose. It was Rome. Polybius now gave all his energy and knowledge to explain how such a large power had come into being. He asserted with pride that Rome's power was the greatest ever achieved—greater than that of Persia or Greece, and that it extended over "almost the whole of the inhabited world" (the expression is used in I. 2 and in several other instances). He also added that it had already lasted longer than any other.

In Greek authors, if anything might be said to resemble the idea of a continuous progress in history, I think it would be this idea of a progressive concentration of power, which is present both in Thucydides and in Polybius. In a way, we might even be tempted to say that, had they been able to see our modern world distributed into great blocks of power, the notion might have appealed to them as a sort of thing they could understand. But they didn't foresee it in the least and their interest in the present left no place for theories about the future. Indeed, Polybius even suggests that no power could be greater than the Roman one (I. 2. 7–8).

This very suggestion of Polybius reveals the limit of this particular kind of optimistic pattern, which supposes a perpetual rise in power. For it was not easy to imagine a larger empire than the Roman one nor one that could last longer. Moreover, as the rest of the world came to be known better, this new knowledge made it still more unlikely that one state should ever, according to Polybius's expression, have command over the whole of it. The result is that, from Roman times to our own, the notion of a continuous evolution or pattern in history had to be shifted from one field to another. It finally applied to the whole of mankind, but then it abandoned the field of states and power to become either religious or spiritual. The very idea of the state has been replaced by such ideas as civilizations or spirit. Philosophers have tried to describe how civilizations could die and yet leave some spiritual acquisition or progress which marked a step in the development of mankind. Rousseau deserves a special mention here for having created a philosophy which considered the history of mankind as a whole and showed freedom as producing the gradual realization of man. Hegel followed a similar course, speaking of the Idea or Spirit, which men gradually conquer through the succession of peoples or civilizations and their eventual rise and fall. Many names of less importance could easily be added.[4]

These philosophers, however, would take us too far away from our theme, and this very circumstance is not devoid of meaning, for it shows clearly the difference in approach and doctrine. The Greeks were not yet interested in civilizations but in practical and political life; and, although they relished general ideas, their political life was too narrow and their attention too much in contact with immediate reality for them to dream of such grand prospects. Also, these prospects rested on a notion that man himself changes, which was quite foreign to them. It is no surprise, then, that no Greek ever ventured to imagine such patterns.

How could they have been so totally pessimistic or optimistic? We owe the Greeks the invention of tragedy, and, if there was one feature that could apply to their view of history as a whole and provide a pattern, I should say it was the tragic feeling and tragic pattern.

The Greeks knew enough history and loved generality well enough to see in history something widely human. But what touched them was not its general course with its optimistic or

pessimistic interpretation. It was what could be called historical contrast—that is to say the actual acknowledgment,
in human events, of the condition of man in its wonderful
greatness and its cruel and inevitable limitations. It was, precisely, the achievement and its ruin. It was rise and fall.

As we have just seen, rise and fall were mingled in the
subject matter of historians, but they were also mingled in
the very existence of man. The Greeks had an acute feeling
that what now rises will sooner or later fall down, that nothing
human ever abides, be it personal prosperity or empires, no
more than human life can go on forever but has to perish.
The very notion of rise and fall seems to be rooted in the inner
sensibility of the Greek—hence the title of this study.

Herodotus was responding to this very feeling when he wrote
in his preface that, among the cities of men, he would speak
equally of the small and powerful ones for, he says, "those
who were big of old have generally become small; and those
who were big in my time were but small on former days: know-
ing that human prosperity never remains in the same place,
I shall mention them both in equal manner" (i. 5).[5]

Indeed, all his great stories are about people who rise and
fall. The opening character in his work is Croesus—Croesus
who thought he was the happiest of men and who was shocked
when Solon told him that nobody could be called happy before
his life had come to an end (i. 32). Now, immediately after
Croesus has received that advice, fortune changes for him and
his power is soon utterly destroyed. When he is on the point
of dying, he remembers Solon and understands, too late, the
meaning of what he had said (i. 86). Then he himself becomes
the adviser. Cyrus, who is at the full height of victory, hears
from him about Solon and remembers that he is after all but
a man and that nothing is ever safe for men. He therefore
becomes suddenly tolerant toward Croesus, whose fate he fears
he might one day experience in his turn, and, precisely, toward
the end of Book i, Cyrus dies the most cruel death—at least
according to Herodotus's narration, which is probably here far
from being correct. Polycrates in Samos is similarly presented

as having risen very high and as having been "too happy"; this is a reason for people like Amasis to fear that this will lead to a miserable end (III. 43). This sad ending arrives when Polycrates dies hanging, in III. 125. And Herodotus comments upon his death, saying: "Such was the end and result of the many good lucks Polycrates had enjoyed—as had been the foreboding of Amasis, king of Egypt." That there are many details in these narrations that don't sound probable from the point of view of accurate history only helps to measure the wish Herodotus had of showing at all costs this pattern of rise and fall in the events he had to recall. Of course Xerxes, at the end of the work, could provide a final example of the same idea.

Thucydides was more critical, but we should never forget that he was writing about the greatness of Athens or at least was organizing his work after this greatness had been ruined. The Funeral Speech, with all its pride and radiance, is set just beside the description of the plague. The trust in victory finds its best expression in Pericles' last speech, which is followed by a comment on his death and the fall of Athens. What is more remarkable, even in this very speech, the idea of an impending doom mingles with lucid confidence for, as Pericles says, "everything that is will, by nature, decay" (II. 64. 3): that is precisely why he is aiming at glory, the only thing that survives when power disappears. In the course of his history, Thucydides himself dwells, with solemn emphasis, on the contrast between Athens's pride at the start of the Sicilian expedition and her utter downfall at the end of it when the Athenians, he says, "considered from what splendour and glory, which they enjoyed before, into how low an estate they were now fallen. . . . For whereas they came with a purpose to enslave others, they departed in greater fear of being made slaves themselves; and instead of prayers and hymns with which they put to sea, they went back again with the contrary maledictions. . . ."[6] The emphasis here is again on the very reversal of fortune, so characteristic of tragedy, and of the Greek view of history.

Nor is this emphasis restricted to the time when tragedy was in full bloom or to its influence. Isocrates insists, with a sort of enjoyment at the clearness of the pattern, on the rise and fall of Athens followed by the rise and fall of Sparta. Later, Demetrius of Phalerum is reported to have been deeply impressed by the way Alexander destroyed the Persians. He says it is a wondrous thought to realize that within fifty years Persia, who was so powerful till then, was to lose even its name, and the Macedonians, then so obscure, would reign over the whole world until fate should decide otherwise regarding the Macedonians.[7] Polybius repeats this saying and marvels at its wisdom precisely when this Macedonian power is, in its turn, destroyed by the Romans.

This is a startling emotion, a Greek and tragic feeling. Its highest expression is to be found in the tears of the conquerors. Toward the end of Polybius's work (xxxviii. 22), Scipio thus sheds tears at his own victory and quotes a line in Homer where Hector says: "A time will come when the holy town of Ilion will perish, with Priam and all the people governed by this brave king" (Iliad vi. 448–49). These tears seem to me to ring the exact note of the Greek feeling with regard to history. They echo, for us, the tears that Xerxes himself, the proud and bold and ambitious conqueror, sheds at the height of his glory, when he beholds the immense extent of his own army: "Then," writes Herodotus, "he congratulated himself on his own happiness, but, after that, started weeping." Being asked about the meaning of such an abrupt change of mood, he answers: "This is because I started thinking and was overcome by pity for the brevity of human life, at the idea that in such a large number of men, none will live more than a hundred years" (vii. 45–46). Weeping in the time of success at the notion that nothing human can last is a kind of response which implies a very close connection between life and death, or rise and fall. One may speak of chance or of the frailty of human prosperity, or one may look for more particular and rational causes. But the feeling is the same, and it doesn't fit in with a philosophy of history which would suppose that any achievement is to last or to remain as a step toward a further and greater achievement.

The true disciples of the classical tradition are, therefore, those who from time to time gave voice to this same emotion. A cold thinker such as Montesquieu expresses this very sentiment when, on occasion, he bursts into exclamations: "Quoi! ce Sénat n'avait fait évanouir tant de rois que pour tomber lui-même dans le plus bas esclavage de quelques uns de ses plus indignes citoyens et s'exterminer par ses propres arrêts! On n'élève donc sa puissance que pour la voir mieux renversée!"[8] Although the eloquence in such a passage is Roman, the keynote and general philosophy can be traced back to the Greeks, for Sophocles wrote, "starry night abides not with men, nor tribulation, nor wealth; in a moment it is gone from us, and another hath its turn of gladness and bereavement."[9]

If there is, then, a pattern in history for the Greeks, it is but the recurrent pattern of rise and fall. However, as a conclusive statement on Greek views of the general course of history, this doesn't leave us on firm ground. It doesn't rule out the idea that some more limited pattern, in each particular case and for each particular state, commands the alternate succession of prosperity and failure, rise and fall, growth and decay.

The very examples just quoted could suggest two such patterns. The first one appears in Sophocles' lines and could be called cyclic. The second one is suggested by Pericles' remark in Thucydides and could be called biological. These two patterns are much closer to the habits of Greek thought than the continuous ones we have considered till now. This doesn't mean that they were accepted as patterns of history—they only came to bear on history after a long time and, even then, vaguely.

The cyclic pattern has been grossly overestimated. If it is true that the Greeks have always been deeply impressed by the order of the cosmos—with the regular evolutions of the sun and moon or of the stars, and with the regular succession,

for men, of nights and days or summers and winters—and if
it is true that they have often used this cyclic order as a starting
point for their cosmologic or cosmogonic representations or even
as a metaphor for their view of human life, there is not one
single instance of a Greek author having developed a cyclic
view of history.[10]

Those who present this view as Greek generally fall back
on the same two authors as before, Hesiod and Plato. Hesiod,
as pointed out before, didn't deal with historical time. It still
remains to be proved that even his mythical notion of ages
is, in fact, cyclic. He says we now live in the Iron Age; the
only possible allusion to a cycle is in line 175, where he wishes
he could have died earlier (that is to say before that age)
or been born later. This seems to imply that things should be
better after the Iron Age. But does it imply that the Golden
Age is sure to take place again? Or does it mean that the
whole series is sure to come back in reverse order, bringing
back, in the end, a new Golden Age?[11] The least one can say
is that such a great hope would then be very poorly hinted at
by this exclamation of sorrow.[12] In a context of myth-related
thought, it is more likely to suppose that the line is vague
and illogical, meaning only that the Iron Age is a terrible age
and one could wish almost anything else. In fact, it sounds
very much as if the myth itself had been put forward for no
other reason than to suggest the hardness of life in the present
age and the impossibility of living without having either the
help of god or the use of *dike* ("justice"). As Vernant says, it
is more a matter of dialectic relation than of chronological succession.[13] It certainly is all but a prediction about the future.

Even Plato, who revels in cycles whenever he deals with
cosmogony, doesn't dare apply that pattern to history. In the
Politicus, no doubt, we have cycles, but then historical time
appears to be but a small part of one of the inverted move-
ments (which are so unhistorical that they change even the
manner in which man's birth is produced). On the other hand,
in the *Republic*, we have history, but no cycle. Plato doesn't
say what tyranny will normally change into—certainly not

into his own ideal constitution—and we should keep in mind the objections raised by Aristotle on this point when he complains of Plato's silence and remarks that tyranny should have to bring back the ideal constitution again if it were to be a cycle (*Pol.* 1316a: συνεχὲς καὶ κύκλος). The conclusion is, I think, obvious: Plato didn't treat that point and didn't speak of a cycle, probably because he didn't think it was one.

In that respect, he differs from Polybius who did take the leap and speak of a cycle, a cycle of constitutions. To Polybius, constitutions have something to do with power, so that he may have had some idea that, during the first constitutions, the state rises, but that it will fall with a corrupted one. Still, his cycle doesn't deal directly with power nor does it seem to be a perfectly clear theory even with regard to constitutions.[14] It is true that it is stated with bold confidence: Polybius uses the emphatic and unclassical word ἀνακύκλω- σις (vi. 9. 10). But this doesn't fit in very well with his own admiration for the exceptional qualities of the mixed constitution prevailing in Rome. Many scholars have tried to deal with the difficulty by supposing successive periods in Polybius's thought. Others find that discrepancies can be reconciled if not pressed with too much precision.[15] An important article on the question suggests that Book vi "is indeed a whole, but it remains a muddled whole."[16] In any case, it seems rather significant that the only Greek author speaking about cyclic evolution should not only limit his scope to constitutions, but that he should be one so ill-qualified for lucidity and firmness in his theoretical analyses.

In fact, only one man in Greece, to my knowledge at least, mentioned the idea of a cycle as related to the rise and fall of human prosperity and power: this is Herodotus. In the Croesus story, his Croesus says: "If you have understood that you are a man and that you reign over men, be aware that human affairs follow a cycle, the circular movement of which doesn't allow the same people to remain always prosperous" (i. 207). The word here is cycle (κύκλος), but the idea is obviously the sheer instability of human life. It doesn't convey any notion of regular evolution. It doesn't explain and doesn't foretell anything about the future. It even precludes all possibility of foretelling anything about it. It is general, wise, unpretending.[17]

This enhances the contrast with those modern authors who did speak of cycles in the history of mankind—this in bold reconstructions, dealing, as we have seen before, not with states but with civilizations. Vico is a good example. He considers threefold elements and ages—divine, heroic, and human—and thus succeeds in finding repetitions or *ricorsi*, such as the beginning of Christianity repeating the Heroic Age, or the Middle Ages repeating barbarism.[18] Another example could be Arnold Toynbee, who explains the rise and fall of all civilizations by the repeated combination of challenge and response. Such reconstructions, generally built up as functions of present experience, go far beyond the possibilities of the Greeks, who couldn't compare so many different histories and whose prudence, perhaps, would not have allowed them to be quite happy with such notions. I am not discussing cyclic time here; but cyclic history is, I may say, in spite of what one might believe, easier to find in modern writing than in Greek thought.

There is one form of cycle, however, which did appeal to the Greeks, because it was rooted in nature and common experience—the biological cycle connecting life and death, growth and decay. According to this pattern, states, like any other being, could be said to have a natural growth leading to maturity and then, inevitably, to decline and fall.[19]

This biological pattern, indeed, underlies all metaphors of rise and fall or growth and decay. It is always implied whenever an author speaks about the ἀκμή of a person or city or uses the cognate verb ἀκμάζειν. Thucydides writes that he immediately knew the Peloponnesian War would be more important than any war before, because the two states were then ἀκμάζοντες in all their force, that is to say they were at the highest point of their development (ɪ. 1. 1). He again repeats that the Athenians were ἀκμάζοντες with great youth (ɪɪ. 20).

He also speaks of the expedition of Athens to Megara, saying it was impressive because the city was still ἀκμαζούσης and had not yet suffered from the plague (II. 31. 2). Such an ἀκμή supposes subsequent decline. According to an idea often repeated in Greece, anything that is born and grows will also decline and die. Anaximander had already said it (fragment B1).

Now it is quite possible that Thucydides, when he wrote about all things being bound to decline, had such a biological pattern in mind, for the verb he uses is πέφυκε, which means that a thing has "grown into being." The idea lingers behind any use of the verb as applied to politics. Yet, there is a great distance between such unavowed implications and a real system, suggesting an unavoidable evolution.

I would say the same about several other passages which show that the idea is never far away but that it is still no more than a metaphor. There is another passage of that kind in Thucydides, when Alcibiades says that "a state as well as any other thing, will, if it rest, wear out of itself" (VI. 18. 6).[20] There is a similar passage in Sophocles, when, in *Oedipus Coloneus*, the state is said not to have grown old (as the chorus has). There is another in the fifth Platonic letter, when the author says Plato found the Athenians already too old to be transformed (322a). There probably are many others, but this in itself has nothing to do with any philosophy of history.

The doctrine becomes a little more assertive and precise in Polybius's time. In that same Book VI, where so many patterns are combined, we find him referring to such an idea as to something well known and commonly approved of: "Any living being," he writes, "or constitution, or enterprise, has, according to nature, its growth, its maturity, and its decay; and everything is at its strongest for those who are in their maturity. This is what then made all the difference between the political achievements of both cities. For Carthage's power and prosperity had begun earlier than Rome's, and was, at that time, past its highest development, whereas Rome was then at her highest point, as regards her constitution" (VI. 51. 4–5).[21]

This is an important idea, and one that was later to have
quite a number of supporters. However, it can only be adopted
for a state which isn't destroyed by defeat, but threatened
by internal decay: the biological pattern is Roman, not Greek.
This is but another proof of the influence political events may
have on political philosophy.

There are quite a number of allusions, in Latin, to the
old age or youth of states. Cicero in the *Republic* offers a
contrast between the young city of Rome and Greece, which is
"prope senescente jam" (i. 38). It is quite probable that both
Cato and Varro had been even more precise.[22] But in any case
we have four well-known and remarkable texts which draw a
close parallel between the different ages of man and the different moments of Roman history. One is a theory attributed
to Seneca by Lactantius (*Div. Inst.* vii. 15); the others are
Florus (i. 5–8), Ammianus (xiv. 6. 3sqq.) and the Historia Au-
gusta (Vopiscus *Vita Cari* 2. 1sqq.). All four are very systematic; they give exact dates for Rome's infancy or adolescence,
and so on. Scholars have been busy studying the differences
between these authors, seeing whether they had any political
implications and reconciling the four texts.[23] For our study,
the only important fact is that they are rather late texts and
not by first-class authors. Once more, the modern age was to
be bolder in its thinking than the former age.[24]

We find the idea in authors as different from one another
as Bossuet and Fontenelle. Then, it occurs once more in Vico,
who speaks (1096) of the way in which all nations develop from
their birth to their decline through all the successive steps mark-
ing the evolution. It has still more importance in Hegel. First
of all, he applies the pattern to particular states and tries to
explain it by natural causes: "When a people is fully grown
up," he writes, "when it has reached its goal, then its deepest
interests fade away. The spirit of a people is a natural individual: as such, it grows, and gets stronger, then decays, and
dies" (*Philosophical History* 1830. ii. 1). But he also adopts
the same pattern for the whole universe, oriental kingdoms
being the childhood of civilization, the Greek world its youth,

and so on. Then, one may ask, what about the notion of a progressive march toward the triumph of the Concept? Hegel can manage that: Ammianus had already admitted that old age meant peace and wisdom, not decay, and the Christians had seen old age as the eve of salvation. Hegel does the same; he says that old age means loss of strength in general, but not for the Concept, whose old age is, in fact, perfect maturity (*The Course of History*, chap. 5).

I should like to stop this brief survey on such a brilliant example. No doubt one can find, cited in the works of those who have studied that pattern, many other modern thinkers—starting with Spengler and Ortega y Gasset. But I think I have said enough to show how the pattern developed progressively, and I hope that the contrast will come out clearly. It is, to me, illuminating. The Greeks never attempted such general applications of their biological pattern. By using it, they only meant to say that things grow and are ultimately destroyed. It was, for them, a simple metaphor. They didn't expect their metaphors to become theories nor did they think these metaphors provided an explanation or could be the basis of any prevision. People, cities, and empires grow and then become impotent and weak. That is a fact. But for the Greeks, this general idea didn't in the least solve the question of how and why they rise or fall (nor did it allow them to predict when they should either rise or fall). This problem remained for them fresh and urgent. They did indeed try to find the answer. Some might be content to think chance turns and changes. Others might think of divine action. Most looked for a human evolution in technics, or policy, or even morality. But all were seeking the reason why: the biological pattern, when it occurred to them at all, was but a way of formulating data, which only stirred their lucidity and intellectual curiosity.

Now this could seem, at first sight, to be the normal approach of all modern historians—a straightforward rather than philosophical approach. Yet, if we look a little more closely into that matter, we soon find that Greek historians behaved, in that search for causes, in a slightly different manner from modern historians. Their attitude presents two particular features which are connected with the biological pattern and with their constant notion that rise and fall are tied to one another in a coherent and unavoidable contrast.

The first of these features is a tendency to look for general reasons applying to many states if not to all. Just as all human beings, or even all living beings, partake in the same evolution from birth to growth and then to death, almost every Greek historian seems to be haunted by the idea that states are submitted to some general conditions which bring out similar evolutions for each of them. Even Herodotus, who is the very last person to indulge in theory or system, alludes occasionally to the dangers of a too high position, or to the stimulus one gets from freedom, or to the natural propensity of a rising power to rise still higher. He doesn't turn these remarks into a general and avowed scheme; he only includes them here and there while dealing with Darius or Xerxes and elsewhere with Athens. But in the most practical and particular anecdotes, or in an isolated piece of advice, he does refer to such general notions and recurrent patterns. Everyone knows that these have become the very core of Thucydides' work and that his supreme art consists in always displaying the general while describing the particular, and describing it with care and accuracy. This is why he intends his work to be of some use for those who will have to deal with later events, "which, according to their human character, will be like the past ones or resemble them." The same spirit and intention can be found in Isocrates who tries to describe the "illness" which overcame and destroyed both Athens and Sparta. It can also be found in Plato, who turns history into a sort of ideal scheme. As for Polybius, he repeats over and over again that his work is meant to be useful in practical life.[25] Whenever he can, or thinks he can, he is happy to draw a general lesson from his own narrative and give it solemn emphasis.[26] Now such a trend of thought is what made it possible for me to try to summarize the ideas of these historians on the rise and fall of states: whenever they spoke of a state, they were either expressing or suggesting a general view about what its actual rise or fall had in common with the fate of others. Indeed, their works hold an intermediate position between the matter-of-fact narration of events which scientific history is often supposed to be and the bold interpretation of them which some philosophers of history have tried to achieve. In that respect, the followers of these historians are people like Montesquieu, Benjamin Constant, or perhaps like Gibbon —not like modern historians from the nineteenth century onward.

But we can go even further, for this recurrent contrast or biological metaphor also suggested to the Greeks the more or less accepted idea that the reasons for growth and decay were most of the time connected with one another and that both growth and decay were but the successive aspects of some inward disposition which commanded their succession.

Plato, as we all know, tried to show that each constitution is brought to an end and destroyed by the very development of its own leading principle, be it honor, or greed, or liberty.[27] It seems to me that Greek historians always thought along similar lines. In Herodotus, rising too high is said to be dangerous; it calls for divine attention and jealous wrath (vii. 10): the sequence of rise and fall is explained in religious terms. In Thucydides, the Athenians, having once started to rise, are caught in a more and more difficult situation. They can scarcely face it without committing mistakes, which this very situation makes all the more dangerous; the sequence of rise and fall is thus explained from a political point of view. In Isocrates, power at sea, that is to say unlimited power, is a sort of illness, for, while it develops, it destroys the very qualities with which it had been acquired. It thus ruined both Athens and Sparta: "thanks to their hegemony on land, and to the good order and energy which they practiced while they had it, the Spartans easily won supreme power at sea; but thanks to the license which this power developed in them, they were promptly deprived even of their former hegemony. . . . They didn't know that supreme power, which everybody longs to acquire, is indeed hard to manage, and that it breeds folly in those who court it, for its nature can be compared with that of the prostitutes, who compel people to fall in love with them, but ruin those who indulge in their intercourse" (*Peace*, 102–3). The sequence of rise and fall is thus explained by a psychological reason. Others have insisted, in a very similar spirit, on the manner in which difficulties and poverty stimulate the people's virtues and make the state rise, thus producing easy life and wealth, which, in their turn, ruin and overthrow the power thus acquired; this is almost an economic explanation. But all these explanations, which we shall examine in the following chapters, have at least one feature which is common to them all: they never establish a contrast between some reasons which account for the rise of a state and others which account for its ruin—they all try to explain both rise and fall as one and the same process, due to the evolution of one and the same situation.

The result is that the great problem of politics, for them, arose from this very connection: they tried to break that connection, to escape and to avoid that more or less fatal evolution; their aim was to stop at the right moment and to find a way of becoming powerful without undergoing the evils attached to power.

Rise and fall are not only linked together in a sort of tragic contrast, illustrating the frailty of human condition and stirring up emotion, but are also connected with one another in a practical and threatening process, which at first stimulates intellectual curiosity and then, as the link becomes clearer, prompts a passionate effort to find a solution and teach it to mankind.

I hope by these preliminary remarks to have somehow cleared the ground for our further inquiry. We shall now be able to try to see what reasons were actually offered by the different authors for the rise and fall of states with less danger of misunderstanding. Moreover, two notions already emerge about these reasons.

The first one concerns their nature. Obviously all Greek authors considered the rise and fall of a state just as they would consider the rise and fall of an individual person. The pattern of rise and fall has nothing to do with states as such, nor did the Greeks conceive any difference in nature between states and individuals. For Plato, they were parallel; and Thucydides likes to draw rules with application, as he says "for a city as for a man."[28] This, of course, is bound to leave out all the explanations founded on political facts as such—namely, economy, demography, social conditions, or the like. The reasons for the rise and fall of states, according to Greek authors, will be mainly moral and psychological.

The second notion which can be derived from what we have seen concerns the problem on which these authors concentrated. What they search for is the reason why the rise of a state turns to its downfall. Therefore, their interest is focused on this turning point; not on the rise, but on its dangers. This explains why one chapter deals with the rise and two deal with its dangers and the possible remedies. There must be a difference of importance between the two parts of that close-knit pair, this difference being, as I hope I have made clear, rooted in the general view of the Greeks as I have tried to describe it.

II

The Conditions of Success

This chapter is entitled "The Conditions of Success," not "The Causes for the Rise of States" because, as we have already seen, the Greeks didn't center their interest on these causes, which were, for them, obvious—any state or individual, if powerful enough, has a natural desire to expand its authority.

The Greeks, therefore, didn't interpret a policy of power as most of us would do nowadays, that is, in terms of economic wants or needs. Such is indeed the modern interpretation of Athenian imperialism: it speaks of corn supplies and of commercial possibilities. The view of the Greeks was different. I am not quite sure that we are right in blaming them for a lack of political understanding. After all, it still remains to be proved that the conditions and psychological attitudes were not, in fact, different from their modern counterpart. Many things do evolve with time. Real historicism should probably reckon with the history of human dispositions, which do undergo modifications from one society to another.

However that may be, it is a fact that the Greeks knew only one cause for seeking power and that was the love of power with all its different forms: love of action, of glory, of security, or of more complete freedom. All these feelings were blended together to produce ambition or *philotimia*. But, even if we adopt this view as a basis, it is still to be noticed that Greek authors didn't say much about it. Although they insisted, in almost all their works or theories, on the dangers of *philotimia* (or *pleonexia*, if they wanted to express the notion

20

with more severity), they very seldom gave a thought to its nature or sources. They didn't say what it was or how it grew. No doubt there are one or two passages describing Athenian *philotimia*, either because this description explained Athens's action during the war or because it could be used as a means of stimulating action against her. An example of the first case could be the Funeral Speech in Thucydides, where Pericles shows the radiant pleasure the Athenians derive from the greatness of Athens and invites them to fight for it and try, by all means, to preserve it forever. An example of the second case could be the analysis the Corinthians give in Book I of Thucydides, when they insist on the troublesome qualities —perpetual activity, boldness, and continued confidence in the possibility of success—which the Athenians are endowed with and which make them so dangerous. But both these texts are just part of the history of the war; one speech is meant to spur the Athenians into action, the other to spur Sparta into war. Although the Corinthians offer something like an explanation when they say Athenian imperialism is the result of Athenian nature, we need not consider that explanation as being very decisive. It explains the style of their *philotimia*, not their *philotimia* itself (Sparta's *philotimia*, for instance, was different).

Indeed, Greek historians are strangely silent on the feelings which account for imperialistic policy. The Persians, in Herodotus, seem to acquire their huge empire by a series of independent moves. The Athenians in Thucydides acquire theirs in a sort of mechanical and unpremeditated way, which they describe as an excuse, but which Thucydides himself seems to adopt as sound historical explanation (I. 99). The Romans in Polybius just protect themselves or others against naughty conquerors who show up in several parts of the inhabited world.

In all these authors the rise comes by itself, thanks to a series of succesful enterprises. The wish to rise exists by itself just as naturally as the wish to survive with which it is so closely related. But these authors were interested in the conditions which enable the rise to succeed.

These conditions can be divided into two main groups. The practical means of victory come first, as being the most obvious, and they display a kind of Ur-sociology of power. Then will come the political means of a victorious action; they will be perhaps even more important and will bring us directly into political philosophy.

The practical means of success were discovered by the Greeks progressively, the two great occasions of discovery being the experience of the city-state in the Aegean, then the Roman Empire in the Mediterranean world, that is to say at the time of Thucydides and the time of Polybius, respectively.

Thucydides has a theory about power and the means of acquiring it. He formulates it with proud insistence as something new which he is the first to set forth and which his generation was the first to discover. In the first chapters about the growth of power in Greece, Thucydides insists on three items: money, navy, and walls—this being a rather startling proof showing how the Greeks could be aware of practical and economic elements when they thought that such elements were actually involved.

But, of course, there is a tremendous difference between money as we see it and as Thucydides saw it. Our historians would, in speaking of money, deal with problems of distribution and classes or of subsistence in peacetime. In Thucydides, there is only one hint about the possibility for the poor of making money through the war whether directly or indirectly, by thus producing some source for future salaries.[1] In all the rest of his work, the only kind of money he considers is money for the war—money for armaments, ships, walls, and military pay. Each victory ends in collecting a tribute which will increase the leading state's treasury but, on the whole, this tribute and this treasury are for war. Power and money are combined in a reciprocal manner, which remains outside of what we call economics.

This importance of money, however, is none the less a significant discovery, and its novelty appears if we compare

Thucydides with Herodotus and with the experience of the Persian Wars.

Herodotus had often mentioned the wealth of the Persians.[2] Aeschylus, in his *Persians*, was no less insistent.[3] Yet the paradox was that the final victory had been won by the Greeks, whose poverty was a classical theme. This theme is clearly formulated in what Demaratus says to Xerxes in Book vii of Herodotus: Greece "is at all times bred in poverty" (102). This poverty, however, is the very reason which accounts for the Greek strength, "for the people have acquired valiance, which is the product of wisdom and a strong law; and with this valiance Greece wards off both poverty and obedience to a master." In other words, the lesson of the Greek victory shows the moral advantage of poverty.[4]

Things have changed with Thucydides. Poverty, for him, still has its advantages. The poverty of Attica explains the fact that Athens always kept the same population and was never a prey to internal strife with all the disastrous results it usually produces. Yet, one doesn't grow greater thanks to poverty. In Thucydides, the Greek victory over the Persians was directly due to the navy, and the Athenians grew greater after this victory because their fleet enabled them to collect tributes from the allies (i. 19). If it is a fact that there was, in Athens, in the second half of the fifth century b.c. quite an important discussion about the compared merits of wealth and poverty (the *Ploutos* is but one instance), Thucydides was clearly on the side of wealth. He also formed a fine theory of the function of wealth in wartime.

Thucydides insists on the fact that Athens turned the tribute into a treasury, a reserve: she thus had both χρημάτων πρόσοδος ("revenue") which regularly maintained her war equipment, and χρημάτων περιουσία ("reserve") always at hand for any emergency.[5] This reserve enabled her to subjugate Samos, for instance, and to besiege Poteidaia until the city surrendered (cf. ii. 13. 3 and ii. 70. 2); it maintained her power against difficulties and ultimately made her stronger.[6] Now, this seems to Thucydides one of the main reasons for the ex-

ceptional power of Athens. Greece, at first, didn't possess such
περιουσία χρημάτων (ι. 2. 2). Minos was the first to organize
an empire with πρόσοδοι (ι. 4), then the new cities, thanks to
naval activity, had more περιουσία χρημάτων (ι. 7. 1). The
Greeks became organized under the leadership of those who
had περιουσίας (ι. 8. 3); later, naval power brought to some
cities more πρόσοδοι (ι. 13. 1; 15. 1). All that suggests a regular progress, which culminates in the Athenian ἀρχή. The city
that, in Herodotus, had saved Greece while being bred in
poverty becomes, in Thucydides, the master of Greece thanks
to her πρόσοδοι and περιουσία. Indeed, in Book ι the calculation about the chances of each city always returns and
insists on this twofold aspect of money.

Archidamos knows that this is the real difficulty for Sparta
(ι. 80. 3, 4). The Corinthians first suggest that a power resting
on money may have some drawbacks (ι. 121. 3); they then
suggest a contribution (121. 5). Pericles has a long analysis
of the great disadvantage of being short of money: it prevents
both distant expeditions and prolongation of war. As for contribution, it is to no great avail: "Reserves can sustain war
better then contributing money under compulsion" (ι. 141. 5).
Later, he delivers a whole speech (in indirect style in Thucydides) about the exact amount of Athens's wealth and revenue.
When Mytilene revolts, everybody mentions the incidence on
the revenue of Athens (ιιι. 13. 5–6; 39. 8; 46. 2–3). When
Decelea is taken, the same idea recurs (ιv. 108. 1). When
Alcibiades suggests that the Spartans should take possession of
Decelea, his idea is that it would stop the coming in of revenues
(vι. 91. 7). In fact, Athens could only be conquered when the
wealth of Persia came to help the Spartans.

This seems as clear as a mathematical demonstration. Yet,
we should beware of appearances. We should notice that, in
the last part of the work, the very notion of the overwhelming
importance of wealth receives less and less emphasis. It is
easy to understand the reason why, since Athens's wealth
was wasted in imprudent policy and lack of cohesion among
citizens. This accounts for the disagreement that seems to

exist between Herodotus and Thucydides. During the Persian
Wars, the wealth of Persia had proved useless against Greece.
But why useless?—because badly used. Persia had too many
men and ships, crowded in a more or less clumsy way: she
had no training, or preparation, or readiness to face difficulty;
also the Greeks resisted with passion.[7] If Persian money got
the better of Athens in the Peloponnesian War, it was the
result of its being used by the Spartan navy and spent according to Alcibiades' shrewd and well-informed advice; also
the Greeks were now against Athens.

Money, therefore, is a condition of success but it is neither
a necessary condition nor a sufficient one because its efficacy
depends on moral energy and political lucidity.

It is a fact that none of the authors following Thucydides
insisted as much as Thucydides on the importance of money.
There may be various reasons. In Athens, there was no more
wealth in the fourth century B.C.[8] Also the simple name of
tribute became hateful to the Greeks and, as a consequence,
the fact of collecting it seemed to be a political mistake. These
two reasons apply to Isocrates. But even later, although the
importance of wealth for war was admitted as obvious,[9] no
historian laid much stress on it. This should be no surprise to
us: Thucydides' work, brimming with the proud discovery of
the importance of money, had turned out to be the proof that
it didn't avail.

The second condition, though, seems to be a more decisive
one: money helps insofar as it enables a state to become master
of the sea, to have what the Greeks called "thalassocracy"—
and thalassocracy is the way to power.

This notion, found in Thucydides, was not quite a discovery. It had been formed as early as the Persian Wars. But
it is remarkable to see it gradually emerging in the Greek
conscience and becoming more and more precise, more and more
obvious. The power of Athens was directly based on it, and
in a way even Athens's collapse in 404 B.C. seemed to afford a
kind of verification.

Herodotus did, from time to time, hint at the importance of being master of the sea.[10] He does so when Megabazos tells Darius to beware of Histiaeus now that he owns a country with wealth and with timber for making ships (v. 23). He does so more clearly when Hecataeus tells his Ionian friends that the only advisable course is to acquire thalassocracy by first laying hands on some treasures existing in the vicinity (v. 36). He does so again for Thasos, who owns ships, revenues, and a wall—all of which seem dangerous to Darius (vi. 46). He does so very firmly when he says that, had Athens come to terms with Xerxes, nobody would have resisted him at sea, and had nobody resisted him at sea, he would have triumphed in Greece, whatever the efforts displayed against him on land (vii. 139).

These are already keen glimpses. In Thucydides, they have become a theory, indeed a firm and lucid theory. Thucydides doesn't only insist, in the first chapters of Book i, on the progress in naval power, as he does for wealth. Practically speaking, both are closely related to one another; money is only useful insofar as it allows naval power. But what is more original, and what he didn't do in the case of money, is to dwell on the idea that naval power cannot be conquered or even seriously weakened.

The texts are all well known. I would like to mention only the two main ones, namely, Pericles' first and last speeches. In his first speech, he underlines the possibilities of sea power, saying that it enables one, whatever harm the enemy may do on land, to go and do harm to him in his own country with far greater efficacy (i. 142. 4). That is, in fact, what Athens did at the beginning of the war. But the analysis is an important one, which brilliantly links power with mobility and sees the main development of war as something independent of the battlefield itself. All modern ideas about navy, and also with time about airforce and missiles, are based on exactly the same idea. Thucydides could be the very first theoretician of modern strategy and armaments.

A second notion appears in the last speech, and it is directly connected with the acquisition or the maintaining of power. Pericles announces quite clearly that sea power means unlimited power: "You think that your empire bears only on your allies, but I say that, of the two divisions of the world accessible to man, the land and the sea, there is one of which you are absolute masters, and on which you have, or may have, the dominion to any extent you wish; for nobody on earth could oppose your sailing with the navy you actually have, be it the great King or any other nation presently existing" (II. 62. 1). This boundless nature of sea power is the really important notion: "to any extent you wish," says Pericles. Of course he means the possibility of sailing wherever one wants rather than the possibility of conquering, but one may quite easily lead to other. The pamphlet by the Pseudo-Xenophon leaves no doubt about it. The author says, like Thucydides' Pericles, that the navy enables one to go and land wherever one wants and then embark again at one's own wish (II. 4). He even adds that the rapidity of movement suppresses food problems and allows more distant expeditions (II. 5). But he also says that all other people have to yield to such supremacy: islands cannot join against the master of the sea because they cannot group with one another (II. 2), and continental countries cannot resist him because they need commercial exchange by sea. Sea power can expand as it wishes—and if it can, generally it will.

This is the reason why Isocrates is so much averse to what he calls τὴν κατὰ θάλατταν ἀρχὴν or τὴν δύναμιν ταύτην.[11] He had known the case of Athenian sea power so clearly analyzed by Thucydides. He also knew of the Spartan experience which followed and the fact that in 404 B.C., as soon as Sparta became mistress of the sea, she ceased to be the city which had fought for the freedom of all others but imposed everywhere her own control and authority; hence his dogmatism and insistence. Sea power, for him, leads to dominion not to hegemony. Destroying all former virtues it will, in the end, cause the fall of the state which has enjoyed it at first but has soon been drawn in by its irresistible course. This we shall see again in the causes for decline and fall.

It is probably also one of the reasons why Plato, hating moral corruption more than anything else, insisted on the necessity of founding the ideal city away from the sea (*Laws* 704–7). No doubt he shows this moral corruption arising directly from the manner of fighting and not from power, but the call for power is certainly one of the features of this injustice which the indulgence in naval activity creates and breeds among people.[12] When the Romans applied Plato's rule to the Carthaginians (or were supposed to do it),[13] their purpose was obviously to prevent their ever rising again to power.

It would seem, therefore, that we are faced here with an important idea and with a theory that all the Greeks readily accepted. Yet, if we go on to the authors who followed, whether immediately or in later times, it is clear that this very notion soon ceased to be as systematic as it had been in the fifth century and in the first years of the fourth century B.C. Demosthenes still complains about the lack of a strong navy, but he complains about many other drawbacks. His very complaint sounds somewhat obsolete for the reason that Philip had started a new form of war on land, which also rested on mobility and quickness—his strategy being something like the motor and tank strategy.[14] Later we again find some indications about the discovery of the importance of the navy for the Romans. Polybius explains the origin of the Roman navy, showing how, during the war against the Carthaginians, the Romans saw they could not do with a situation in which the Carthaginians could harm Italy without ever being subjected to similar treatment (I. 20)—that is the old Athenian idea. He goes on with the progress in naval warfare: there are good arrangements (I. 26), but disappointments (I. 39; I. 44), then new efforts again (I. 59; 61), the success of which brings Carthage to terms. Indeed, in the second Punic War, Scipio Calvus wins victory at sea (III. 96). In the third, the Romans are in Carthage with a fleet and destroy the city. Yet this is but a minor theme in Polybius's work.

What had been obvious for the Greek cities in the Aegean and in Thucydides' account of the Athenian growth remained a useful experience, but ceased to be a decisive one. Sea power was still considered as a necessary condition, but it ceased to appear as a sufficient one. Again, the practical condition of success which had once appeared as the direct way to power was later integrated into a more complex notion and the emphasis was laid, not on one means among others, but on the moral energy and intelligence which commanded the use of them all.

The same remark could be made about a third element, which didn't yet have pride of place in Thucydides but which still belongs to a first approach to what could be called the sociology of power. This third element is the nature of armament.

Thucydides, as was only natural according to his general theory of war, discussed sea armament and sea tactics. With regard to land operations, he is less interested. He explains the strategy of battles, dwells on discipline, remarks from time to time on technicalities such as the tendency for each army to swerve toward the right (v. 71. 1). He is also interested in the problems of besieging a city and has sometimes more details in that field than in other forms of warfare. But he never goes into practical description and is of little use for sociological analysis. He speaks of armaments as Herodotus spoke of sea power—occasionally and in passing.

Xenophon has more details: more about discipline, more about cavalry, more also about the organization of the Spartan troops. But this is nothing compared with what we have in Polybius, for in his work victory doesn't appear only as the result of discipline and tactics, one resting on the other, but as the result of the specific quality of armament—and that is something new. In Book II (33), he insists on the difference between the two kinds of swords, those of the Gauls and the Romans, and on the practical consequence the difference could have. Similarly, in Book VI (25), he compares the shape of the spears used in Rome and in Greece. In the same Book VI,

he has more than twenty pages on the structure and organization of the Roman camps as opposed to Greek camps (27–42).
In Book XVIII (28–32), he again draws a parallel between the
Roman phalanx and the Macedonian one. "It would be useful
and interesting," he says, "to analyze the difference in method,
in order to try to see what made the Romans superior and
gave them the advantage in the battlefield: thus we shall not
be tempted to consider success as the result of chance" (28).[15]

These are interesting remarks and reveal a new interest.
Both Bossuet and Montesquieu, when speaking about Roman
victories, follow Polybius or quote him.[16] But important as
this new interest may be, it is obvious that the novelties in
armament, even for Polybius, are but part of man's intelligence
in warfare and that the art of war itself still rests on moral
qualities and on training.[17] The differences in armament are
not yet important enough to rule out other elements.

Moreover, armaments depend on the use one makes of
them, and a victory on the battlefield depends on strategy
and on politics as a whole. This leads us to the second group
of conditions, the political conditions of success, which are by
far the most important for Greek authors, although they are
often ignored by modern authors. Perhaps, instead of the political conditions of success I should say the political conditions
for the use and preservation of success. The great problem,
as we have already seen, is to avoid the mistakes that lead to
decline and fall. But it comes to the same; for, ultimately,
decline and fall come through defeats, which are the result
of a wrong or imprudent policy.

Now, are there any conditions for a good policy? Are there
elements which produce it or prevent ordinary mistakes? For
a Greek, the answer to that question was simple: inner conditions can be described as the *politeia* of a state, as its political life and constitution.

As everybody knows, the Greeks loved discussing constitutions. But there is a tendency nowadays to believe that this was
a sort of philosophical discussion, quite free from practical con-

siderations, whereas I think it started in relation with power: the Greeks progressively discovered the advantages and drawbacks of democracy and invented with increasing precision a type of constitution that would be fit for the acquisition and maintaining of power. This time, the line that leads from Herodotus to Thucydides and from Thucydides to Polybius is a continuous line of discovery and progress.

Herodotus had a firm though rather general idea about such matters. In the dialogue between Xerxes and Demaratus, he insisted, as noted before, on the fact that Greece was small and poor, but could all the same be victorious. Why was that?—because, in Greece, the law was a self-imposed rule which everybody obeyed with total devotion: "When in group, they are the bravest of all men; for, if they are free, they are not free in everything: they have a master, the law, which they dread even more, and much more, than your people dread you: they do what it tells them to do and it tells them the same thing always, not allowing them to run away from the battle, whatever the number of the people they have to fight, but telling them to remain at their post and be victorious or die" (vii. 104).

Law, then, is the key and, thanks to the law, there is discipline and heroism. But what law? We find in Herodotus another and more precise idea, namely, that democratic institutions are the best conditions for the rise of a state, because in a democracy every single citizen feels directly responsible for the success of the state and is directly interested in its success. He says it in Book v when dealing with Athens and her liberation from tyrants, for he remarks in chapter 78 that: "when governed by tyrants, the Athenians were not superior in war to any of their neighbors, but once they were free from tyrants they became the first by far. This proves clearly that, while they were kept in obedience, they were easily cowards, because they toiled for a master, whereas, when free, each single person was full of zeal, as toiling for himself."[18] This is not an isolated case: as Herodotus, who is not lavish of generalities, remarks, this advantage of equality shows οὐ κατ᾿ ἓν μοῦνον, ἀλλὰ πανταχῇ not in one instance, but in all cases. Such a theory is supported by Hippocrates when he writes, in his treatise *Airs, Waters, Places* (23): "For, as I have said above, where there are kings, there must be the greatest cowards. For men's souls are enslaved and refuse to run risks readily and recklessly to increase the power of somebody else. But independent people, taking risks on their own behalf and not on behalf of others, are willing and eager to go into danger, for they themselves enjoy the prize of victory. So, institutions contribute a great deal to the formation of courageousness."[19]

Now, this suggestion of Herodotus has an echo in Thucydides and becomes, in his work, a little more precise. I am alluding to the well-known analysis of Pericles' Funeral Speech, when Pericles says he will describe "by what practice and with which *politeia* or ways of life" Athens rose to her greatness and when he goes on with a development on Athens's freedom and ready activity, two qualities of which her actual power is to him the result and the proof (II. 36. 4; 41. 2). One can say this idea is more precise than that found in Herodotus, as Thucydides describes not only freedom as opposed to tyranny, but one particular *politeia* as opposed to that of the Spartans. Also, the result is to him power, that is to say something which depends on a general policy, not only on courage or success in the battlefield.

Yet, one must confess that the analysis runs on very general terms and that it is, in Thucydides' work, rather isolated. In fact, this idea of the advantages of democracy was soon to be corrected when Athens's power was put to trial and discussed. The work as a whole is therefore more a rectification of Herodotus's confident statement than a confirmation, more an answer than an amplified echo.

Indeed, experience here was rich and various during the Peloponnesian war. Professor Woodhead made it the main theme of his book, *Thucydides and the Nature of Power*, where he considers in three different chapters the function of the people, the elite, and the individual.[20] I shall not discuss such theories here, but will keep closer to the text of Thucydides or of his contemporaries in order to see exactly how the progress took place and the idea evolved.

First, it soon became obvious that Athens's power, being a sea power, didn't rest so much on the citizens' courage in the battlefield as on the sailors' training. This meant quite a different link between sea power and democracy.[21] Since the sailors belonged to the lower classes, the emphasis on sea power tended to stress the importance of one fraction of the citizens as opposed to the other. Very soon it appeared that sea power involved the loss of aristocratic virtues, and people of aristocratic tendencies resented it deeply; this is true of the Pseudo-Xenophon, of Isocrates, and of Plato.

From a political point of view, however, even the democrats soon noticed that, if democracy was stimulating for the energy of the people, it was not quite so beneficial either for the general management of war or for the quality of political decisions.

That a one-man command is better for war had been noted as early as Homer (*Iliad* ii. 204–6). In the Peloponnesian War, it appeared in the differences not of states but between groups of states. Pericles, in Thucydides, explains that one of the drawbacks of the Peloponnesian confederacy is that it does not leave the decisions to a single leader and is thus prevented from achieving anything with ready speed (i. 141. 6). Later Demosthenes again was to complain of the same difficulty which made things unequal between Athenian democracy and Philip's possibilities: "He had plenty of money," he writes, "and did what he thought fit, without announcing it beforehand in decrees, without discussing it publicly, without being called in trial by sycophants, without being accused of illegal behavior, or being responsible to anybody, but he was the only master, leader, and supreme authority. Whereas I, who was opposed to him (it is only fair to examine that point), where was my supreme authority? I had none."[22]

But this military difficulty could not be helped and it never became for the Greeks a real problem. On the contrary, the history of the Peloponnesian War reveals a very urgent problem and passionate discussion which arose when the drawbacks of democracy for political decisions were suddenly brought to light.

Cleon, in Thucydides, begins his speech in Book III by a bitter complaint: "In several occasions," he says, "I had already understood that democracy is incapable of commanding an empire" (37. 1). Now, one must admit that such an example is not a very safe one; Cleon is not to be considered a wise man, and the position he is defending is even more unwise, for he means to condemn the unsteadiness of the people, who want to retract their former cruelty to Mytilene—and to retract it quite rightly. But Cleon's analysis of the irresponsible character of assemblies, of the dangers of rhetoric and flattery, is an old and sound notion. Often in Thucydides' discussions, the speakers use correct arguments to defend a wrong thesis. It is a fact that Cleon's criticism of democratic habits and his insistence on the dangers they involve find an echo in Thucydides' own judgment, as stated in Book II. 65. There he says clearly that the demagogues flattered the people, who therefore made the wrong decisions, and he adds: "The result was a great number of mistakes, as was wont to happen in the case of a great city commanding over an empire . . ." (II. 65. 11). These cumulative mistakes end in the final collapse of Athens's power.

Democracy, therefore, is better than tyranny insofar as people are directly interested in their own victory and greatness, but democracy is also dangerous since the people, or the mob, are easily fooled or mistaken.[23] This experience was the starting point of a whole series of reflections and programs in the fourth century B.C.

The simplest solution was, of course, to remember that Periclean democracy had been the rule of one man, as Thucydides has clearly said, and to remember also what Homer and Herodotus had said about the efficacy of one man's rule. The idea lingers and recurs in the fourth century B.C. Isocrates repeats it, giving the example of Sparta in his *Nicocles* (23).

Like Xenophon, he addresses kings, admires kings; gradually, the Hellenistic monarchy is being prepared and approached.

But even without going to that extent, it is a fact that we see the Greek authors of the fourth century B.C. (and of the late fifth century B.C.) turn with obstinacy toward a reform of democracy and toward the institution of a moderate democracy, of the *patrios politeia*, the constitution of their ancestors. Also, one of their major arguments is that this reform will help the very rise of the state.

As early as 411 B.C., Thrasymachos recommended the *patrios politeia* by showing the mishaps and disorders democracy had brought to the city (B l. 17, 26). But the idea gets much clearer after the ruin of Athens. Isocrates insists, in many passages, on the fact that the reasonable constitution of old had allowed Athens to rise, whereas her excesses and disorders (which were due to sea power) had caused her downfall. That is the reason why, although primarily interested in foreign politics, he had to write once about political reform and ask for a return to the moderate constitution of the past. He couldn't do otherwise, for the two questions were directly connected. As he says, "Prosperous situations, everybody knows it, are attained and maintained not by those who have the most beautiful and large fortifications, or by those who can group the greatest number of men, but by those who have, in their state, the best and wisest administration. For the very soul of the city is indeed its constitution [*politeia*], which has there the same power that the mind has in human bodies. It is the constitution which decides everything, and manages to keep what is good, while avoiding accidents, . . . and it is necessary that the situation should conform to what the constitution is" (*Areop.* 13–14).

"Constitution", in such a passage, is an inadequate translation: *politeia* means, as it did in Thucydides, a way of life and policy more than practical institutions. But the way of life and policy are, no doubt, connected with institutions; the very fact that Isocrates mentions one or two technical reforms

shows that the notion of the significance of institutions was
gradually gaining importance.

This leads us to the time when an analysis of institutions
was given as the explanation of the rise and fall of states,
which is the case at the end of our series, that is to say, in
Polybius. Polybius lays all the emphasis on that notion whenever he formulates the aim of his own work—which he does
quite often. "Who is so mean and indifferent as not to wish
he could understand how, and through what kind of *politeia*,
practically all the inhabited world fell, in less than fifty-three
years, under the Roman rule?" This he asks in Book ı. 1. 5;
but he repeats the idea and the very words, first in Book vı.
2. 2, then at the conclusion of his work, in Book xxxıx. 8. 7.
Other formulas are no less insistent: "Whatever can be the
reason, one could ask, why, having subdued all countries and
being far more superior now than before, the Romans couldn't
man as many ships and raise as powerful expeditions as they
used to? The reasons for that will come out clearly when we
shall get to the analysis of the *politeia*" (ı. 64. 1); "I shall then
make a digression, in order to analyze Rome's constitution,
and shall there demonstrate that the particular form of her
political life didn't only play a great part in her acquiring
dominion over the people of Italy and Sicily, and then extending
it to Spanish and Celtic people, but also explains, after her
victory over the Carthaginians, her planning to lay hands on
the whole world" (ııı. 2. 6); "The organization of the constitution is the main cause of success or the reverse in any enterprise" (vı. 2. 9); "This is why this particular form of political
life happens to be irresistible and to reach any aim one pur-
sues" (vı. 18. 4). The formulas are numerous, similar, insistent.
Polybius feels that is the real originality of his work, for the
authors of particular histories cannot grasp, he says, "by what
means and what kind of *politeia* fate produced the most startling achievement of our times" (vııı. 2. 3).[24]

How does the Roman *politeia* come to have such influence?
The analysis which fills the whole of Book vı makes it quite
clear: the Roman constitution is a mixed one, where three dif-

ferent powers and orders are combined—consuls, senate, and people. Now this allows Rome to have both the advantages Herodotus saw in freedom and those Isocrates saw in a more aristocratic and controlled government than the Athenian democracy of the late fifth century B.C. As Polybius explains, whenever there is an emergency, the three powers agree and every single person is directly interested in the common success and is responsible for it (VI. 18. 2: συνεργεῖν ἀλλήλοις; 3: ἑκάστου συνεργοῦντος); hence, rapidity and efficacy. But when security and prosperity might turn out to be dangerous, as they generally do (ὃ δὴ φιλεῖ γίνεσθαι), the different powers act as a sort of brake to one another, preventing the pride and ambition which might arise in any of them (5–8).[25] Thus the natural evolution leading from rise to decline and fall is either stopped or postponed.[26]

Indeed, Polybius shows, with emphasis and obvious satisfaction, how it works. The place in which he mentions and describes the Roman constitution is a far from indifferent choice. Apart from the chapters of introduction or the justification of his general structure, he first mentions it at the end of Book III, after the battle of Cannae when the Romans had not only lost their dominion over Italy, but feared the worst while they awaited Hannibal's arrival. But in spite of that (III. 118. 7: οὐ μὴν), the Senate left nothing undone of what was to be done, but stimulated the courage of the people, so that "thanks to the particular form of their political life, they not only resumed their power over Italy after having had the better over the Carthaginians, but soon became the masters of the whole inhabited world." Immediately thereafter comes the announcement that Polybius will later give an analysis of that *politeia*. But "later" means later in the work, not later in time. Books IV and V deal with the affairs in Greece and Asia; at the end of Book V, he comes back to Italy and to the situation after Cannae, where he had left his readers at the end of Book III. Then comes the analysis of Book VI—a whole book of political analysis, which is remarkable enough.

At the end of that book, he arrives at Rome's stupendous energy in recovering from the blow she had received, and he also explains the first decision of the Senate. Some Roman prisoners get to Rome and beseech the Senate to agree that all the Roman prisoners should be liberated under ransom; but the Senate, in spite of the dramatic situation which then prevailed (and which Polybius eloquently recalls) refuses to do so. The Senate, indeed, feared that the Romans would fight with less energy than if they knew they could only conquer or die (vi. 58). The firmness of the people was stimulated by the wisdom and energy of the Senate. The turning point of Rome's power is thus an illustration of what this "mixed constitution" could do.[27]

I am not going to discuss, after so many scholars, whom Polybius borrowed this theory from or what its shortcomings are in regard to Roman history. But whatever its origins or sources may be, I think it is obvious, from the passages I have just mentioned, that the theory arose quite naturally from the reflections on power made in the preceding period. It was the most natural answer to the problem previously dealt with, for it could account at the same time for the acquisition of power through courage and energy and for its preservation through wisdom and clear-sighted firmness. If it sounds, in some ways, oversimplified, sometimes inadequate, or out of focus, that is because the aim was not so much to describe the Roman reality in its specificity than to answer a long-debated question that had matured in a series of authors—authors of whom I have mentioned only the most noteworthy among those whose works have been preserved.

However, one conclusion emerges from that long series of texts, developing a theory that was to have such influence on classical reflection:[28] it is that, although the great theoreticians like Plato or Aristotle never insisted on power and were even afraid of its possibilities, the very notions they dealt with had been, in the first instance, discovered in the name not of justice but of power and according to the practical experience of successive empires.

Yet important as these successive discoveries may have been, we must be aware that even for Polybius, even for the man who was proud of asserting a new view about history, this notion about constitutions does not mean that the main reasons for the rise and fall of states were ultimately political; for him, as for all Greek authors, they were not political, but moral.

Indeed, we should always keep in mind that, for all Greek authors, *politeia* is something much wider and more general than our "constitution." What Thucydides describes in the *Epitaphios* as the means by which Athens achieved her greatness is summed up in the three words, *epitedeusis, politeia, tropoi*—a moral vocabulary. Nothing in his description deals with institutions as such. Isocrates similarly speaks of "everyday life and practices in general" (*Areop.* 61: *epitedeumasi*), and no doubt he suggests one or two possible reforms. He also mentions the choice of magistrates along with these "general practices," but the main bulk of his treatise bears on education, virtue, and general morality. An innocent reader could very well remain unaware of the political suggestions that accompany these great themes. Dionysus of Halicarnassus will similarly speak of the *epitedeumata* by which Rome obtained her power.[29] Now, Polybius no doubt is a little more technical, and that is where his originality lies. But even for him, and even in Book VI, institutions are far from being all. The discussions on armaments earlier in the chapter belong there. Toward the end of the book, when he compares the Roman and Cretan *politeiai*, he says himself that there are two principles which make a *politeia* good or bad: those are ἔθη and νόμοι, moral habits and laws.[30] Indeed, even when he speaks of institutions it is obvious that they can only be of some good insofar as they help preserve moral standards, whatever the situation. Rome, in a crucial moment behaved, thanks to her institutions, according to courage and energy. Those are virtues. There are other virtues as well, for he shows that the Spartan constitution lacked a system preventing the city from greed and cruelty in her behavior toward her neighbors.[31] A constitution is good when it enables a state to display the various virtues that lead to its rise and greatness. All political writings, in Greek civilization, deal only with virtues; their presence or absence is the only reason for the rise and fall of states.

But the example just mentioned—the example of Sparta—calls our attention to a last remark. What were those virtues which a good *politeia* was to breed among the citizens and which would produce or maintain the greatness of the state? Polybius insists only on some of them. He speaks about cases of emergency and about courageous decisions. In times of prosperity, other qualities are required. Polybius doesn't insist on them, perhaps, but his general formulation includes them and they can be read in his work, as we shall later see. These qualities are those that enable the state to oppose the natural evolution leading from success to moral corruption, and thence to decline and fall.[32] In other words, they are mostly negative and they rest on self-control; they enable people not to be effeminated by wealth, divided by personal ambition, or carried too far by national ambition. The so-called constitution helps in fostering these virtues, but it cannot produce them directly. Once more, it comes in as a condition, as a favorable element—not as the ultimate and sufficient cause or explanation.

I hope these sucessive distinctions have made it clear that, although the Greeks gradually discovered and analyzed several elements leading to the acquisition and preservation of power, they didn't think they had thus gone to the bottom of the question. Each practical experience was turned into an intellectual discovery, which changed the very substance of historical writing. But there is always something else lurking behind these successive discoveries, something which all these authors accepted as obvious and as all-important so that, in a way, we have not yet approached our problem in its more important aspects.

What we have seen is, first, that the Greeks were not totally ignorant of practical matters and conditions. I could, in fact, have added other proofs. I could have argued that the Greeks didn't ignore even those factors—such as demographic and social conditions—which would nowadays have pride of place. As early as the fifth century B.C., they knew about the difficulties arising for Sparta from her restricted population (ὀλιγανθρωπία), or from her fear of inner revolts, caused by the subdued condition of hilots. They also knew about the problem of work and war (when Pericles spoke about the Spartans being αὐτουργοί). They also had discussions about the best size for a town. They knew about many things. But what else we have seen is that, though they knew about these factors as about many others, they didn't choose to put the emphasis on them. Their insistence on moral notions acquires, by contrast, an even greater importance.

The result is that, at the end of this chapter, we are finally brought back to the psychological attitudes with which we began. This is, for once, a cycle—or perhaps it isn't. We have found, at the root of the state's rise toward power, a natural disposition of the people to activity, ambition, and energy. What we find at the end, as the essential means of retaining power, is a lucid effort to combine courage, wisdom, and self-control, so as to escape the risk of a natural temptation. We have not *phusis* but *ethos*, and an organized and responsible *ethos*, almost a sort of national *paideia*. Indeed, energy and ambition either are possessed or are not possessed, but political wisdom and firmness can be taught by experience and lucidly managed in a good state. The two following chapters therefore will describe the way in which this lesson was received and understood.

This attitude is deeply characteristic of the Greek effort toward *politikê aretê*. People like Machiavelli or Montesquieu were still obeying that inner aspiration. The sociology of power has but recently replaced, and partly replaced, the pedagogy of good policy, resting on man's morality and responsibility.

III

Hybris *in* *Politics*

The most obvious link between rise and fall, in Greek thought, can be summed up in the word *hybris*. Prosperity fosters *hybris* —ambition and the wish to have more than one's share—and disaster soon follows. But why is disaster the result? The first answer to that question is a religious one: *hybris* is punished by the gods, who hate such excess on the part of man. This explanation soon gave way to others of a more rational and political nature, which were born from experience and reflection. Although the idea sounds like a very old and simple cliché, it will thus be easy to see that its development, in Greek historians, implies a whole series of changes and discoveries to which more modern authors may still be indebted. This series of discoveries is a long one, and runs through all Greek literature, but the boldest progress, and the decisive one, is to be found in Thucydides. What his followers added to his analysis are only slight changes and complements. Indeed, the problem as he had diagnosed it and formulated it was so clear and urgent that they were primarily concerned with trying to find solutions. In this chapter I shall, except for a few anticipations, deal only with Herodotus, Thucydides, and their contemporaries. In the second section of the chapter, I shall trace three different ways in which the decline of civic morality comes to bear on politics.

Herodotus has given the clearest definition of *hybris* one could desire. What is of equal interest is the fact that he has given it in connection with the Persian enterprise against Greece, when the power of the Persians was severely shaken and their rising forever stopped. Before Xerxes made his final decision, Artabanus tried to prevent him from attacking Greece. Among other arguments, he offered: "You see the biggest creatures, how God crushes them with his thunder, and doesn't allow them to make a show of their great size? but the small ones don't trouble him. You see how he always directs his blows toward the highest houses and the highest trees. God indeed abases anything that grows above the rest. . . . For God doesn't allow high-mindedness in others but himself" (vii. 10). This is clear and neat. A house, or a man, or an empire is crushed because it has become great. It cannot be helped. Perhaps that is precisely what happened to Xerxes, for Artabanus will explain shortly afterward that, when he was speaking against the war, he was trying to oppose the view in which he saw *hybris* (vii. 16).

In any case, this is also a very old formulation, which Aeschylus already called παλαίφατος and γέρων in *Agamemnon* 750 ff., and which his avowed moralism strongly objected to: "Apart from others I think by myself: no, it is the impious deed which begets others of the same kind, for, in rightful houses, fate has but a beautiful off-spring."[1] In fact this old and simple creed is so simple that even Herodotus cannot be credited with it. This is what I should like to call attention to; and first, we must acknowledge that the notion which appears in his work is just a shade more subtle.

Let us consider the Croesus-Cyrus episode, which is so often quoted as showing the hand of God in history—a hand which abases with unpredictable disaster the most prosperous beings, thus reminding us all of how precarious any prosperity ever is. Yet, even here, we may notice a very precise commentary, given by Herodotus. What irritated the gods was not the importance of Croesus's prosperity, but the thoughts which it inspired him with: "Divine wrath fell heavily on Croesus, apparently because he had thought himself the happiest of all men" (i. 34). It is a thought which the gods punish, not a situation. If we look at the manner in which they brought

on the fall of Croesus, we see that the means consisted of two
oracles, which Croesus, in both cases, equally misunderstood
because he was too optimistic about his own happiness—so
optimistic that he didn't act, says Herodotus, as a man who
is to make a wise decision (I. 91: εὖ μέλλοντα βουλεύσεσθαι).

Artabanus himself, who provided us with the old and simple
formula we started with, does think along similar lines. He
speaks of divine wrath as acting against high thoughts, not
against great powers. He also adds a most interesting remark,
for he says: "Haste in action begets false steps (σφάλματα),
which generally produce great damage; whereas there is advantage in taking one's time" (VII. 10). Similarly, just before
he mentions *hybris* in the other passage, he insists on the importance of a wise decision (δ,ε : εὖ βουλεύεσθαι). The pattern of rise and fall in Herodotus has its warrant in God's
intervention, but the link is provided by overconfidence and
by imprudence.

We thus get an opening toward a more thorough analysis.
First, prosperity creates overconfidence and offensive action
(this idea is indeed repeated in III. 80. 4 as regards individuals,
for the virtuous man is said to change as soon as he acquires
supreme power: *hybris* develops in him as a result of his high
position). The mistake and doom are but the distant product
of such an attitude. The pattern is thus not so simple as Artabanus has described it to Xerxes—whether prompted by
shrewd flattery or only obeying proverbial tradition. Herodotus's pattern is a more rationalistic one and a more satisfactory
one as regards morality; still, with these corrections, it remains clear and neat. Only, in my opinion at least, Herodotus
didn't keep to that pattern either and never laid stress on it.

God destroyed Croesus's overconfidence, that is true. But,
ultimately, it appears that this overconfidence was not the
real cause: the Delphic priestess herself explains that Croesus
pays for a fault of his ancestor in the fifth generation (I. 91).[2]
This is justice—justice in its most archaic features—but it is
not that particular kind of justice which may show in the
system of *hybris* and *nemesis*.

As for Xerxes, if he may be suspected of overconfidence, this does not have much to do with his disaster; his overconfidence has a good excuse, for he needs a dream, and a repeated dream, which Artabanus, although skeptical at first, can see as well as the king had, before he accepts the idea of starting the expedition. He is not guilty of *hybris*, but is deceived in spite of his prudence and in spite of the fear he has of *hybris*.

Now, it is impossible for us to know whether Herodotus believed in this story about the dream: he says what the Persians say (vii. 12. 1: ὡς λέγεται ὑπὸ Περσέων). But, by inserting it in his narration of events, he ruins the pattern of *hybris* and *nemesis*. It is hard to see whether he suggests another one in its place. From the story itself, nothing can be inferred. It could be an excuse for Xerxes or it could be a sign that the gods were against him. But why against him?— the archaic justice which was to be found in the case of Croesus and which is, in fact, mentioned for Xerxes in Aeschylus's *Persians* is here totally unknown: no previous fault of some ancestor is hinted at, no condemnation of Xerxes' family is supposed.

Indeed, Artabanus's theory of *hybris*, whether in its simplest form or in its more elaborate shape, is not once supported by Herodotus's history. No theory, in fact, is supported by Herodotus, not even the most modest of all, which explains the wrath of God by a religious fault. No doubt such a theory would not effectively explain the rise and fall of states; but still the hand of God could trace a legible pattern—as it does in Aeschylus or as it will do in Augustine or Bossuet. But does it?

Impious deeds are occasionally punished in Herodotus.[3] Such an explanation is the most obvious one when a man sinks into madness and suicide, as does Cleomenes. Indeed, Herodotus in that case mentions three different explanations, all three of which link his ruin with some sort of impiety (vi. 75); this proves that the notion was commonly held. The historian chooses one himself, thus accepting this very trend of thought. But then he is careful to mention at the end another and more realistic explanation resting on the use and abuse of wine.[4] Once again he proves very keen on information and story telling but, for that very reason, rather indifferent to historical patterns as such.

If this is clear in the case of Cleomenes, how much clearer still it is with Xerxes. Xerxes was responsible for impious deeds. He offended Poseidon while crossing the Hellespont (vi. 35); then again he offended Apollo when his troops attacked Delphi (viii. 36–39); and he offended all the gods when his troops burned Athens (viii. 53).[5] Herodotus is careful to mention all these actions. But, if we compare Aeschylus's *Persians*, we can measure the difference: in Aeschylus, these deeds are the main reason for Xerxes' ruin, whereas in Herodotus, no connection is ever suggested, not even by a hint. We can read it in his text if we want, but we certainly don't do it with much encouragement from him.

We can read in his work many other explanations, and much more forcible ones, of the rise and fall of Persia. In regard to the latter, or to be more exact the defeat of Persia,[6] the lack of freedom and of naval training has already been mentioned. To this must be added the reflections Artabanus offers about the difficulty of prudence, for his speech rests on a long analysis of the military situation and of former experiences. Professor Immerwahr has shown that political explanations were far from absent in Herodotus's work.

However that may be, the least one can say is that Herodotus, although he occasionally puts forth general notions about religious *hybris*,[7] shows a clear tendency to adopt more rationalistic explanations and attitudes by which he is—*volens nolens*—paving the way for Thucydides and for a totally political *hybris*.

Political *hybris* provides a pattern which is just as clear and neat as religious *hybris*. One is exalted by success, the more so if it is an unexpected or sudden success; ambition then disregards prudence and overconfidence brings out failure.

This is another well-known pattern. We find it in Thucydides as a course that one should beware of following.[8] We find it also in several other authors. I would like to quote one instance, namely, the famous passage of the *Suppliant Women*, where Euripides speaks of the conqueror who, after having caused the ruin of his enemy, "is like a poor man who has just become rich: he commits *hybris*, and his *hybris* causes him to be ruined in his turn."[9] Now, if Thucydides had only provided this more rationalistic pattern and insisted, as Euripides does, on the mechanism of such temptation, it would indeed be an important progress. But it would not be a very deep analysis. The force of his analysis comes from the fact that he links this simple pattern with a lucid reflection on the very nature of power.

Power is unwelcome to those who don't have it, and a state which commands over others becomes an object of fear and hostility or even hatred. This is emphatically repeated in all the speeches of Thucydides. The enemies of Athens, of course, mention the fact as a reason for war and a hope for victory. But, what is more remarkable, all Athenian speakers also dwell on the idea, which serves as an explanation of their policy. The Athenians in Book ι say they are hated (ι. 76. 1: εἰ . . . ἀπήχθεσθε ἐν τῇ ἡγεμονίᾳ ὥσπερ ἡμεῖς ; I. 77 : ἡ δὲ ἡμετέρα ἀρχὴ χαλεπὴ δοκεῖ εἶναι, εἰκότως). Pericles repeats it even more clearly when he says (ιι. 63. 2): "What is at stake is not only slavery or freedom, but the loss of your empire and the danger which arises from the hatred you have encountered in that empire; as for this empire, you cannot get away from it . . . you hold it as a tyranny, which it seems injust to acquire, but dangerous to let out." Cleon echoes Pericles, but with still more insistence: "You don't realize that your empire is a tyranny, that you command over people who plot against you and are your subjects against their own will: they don't obey you for the sake of the favors you may indulge in toward them at your own prejudice, but because of a superiority which you owe to sheer force more than to their good-will" (ιιι. 40. 3). The Athenians in Melos declare that independent people are considered to remain free as long as they have power enough to inspire fright (v. 97) and that those

under command are provoked by constraint (v. 99). Alcibiades
speaks of the natural fear and preventive action prevailing
among independent people and of the necessity of acting against
them in order to maintain the authority of Athens over
others (vi. 18. 3).

This insistence is remarkable but the notion itself should
not cause surprise. This condition, so firmly repeated in Thucydides, was indeed acknowledged by all contemporary authors,
beginning with the Pseudo-Xenophon and going down to Isocrates. An attempt has been made recently to prove that
such a view was wrong and rested on bias. This attempt was
made, in my opinion, without reason or success.[10] But even
if there were some bias, which I don't believe, the fact remains
that such is the basis of Thucydides' thought about the rise
and fall of Athens.

This very condition is what bids both for *hybris* and for
its dangers. If the Athenian speakers all mention that condition, it is because it presses Athens toward becoming more
and more powerful. Being an object of fear and suspicion on
one side, of hatred and plots on the other, obliges the conquer-
or to make a display of his own force, that is to say to be
aggressive whenever he suspects a possible action against him
and to be always severe whenever a subject seems bold enough
to revolt. The first attitude is given as explaining the war,
which Pericles recommends as a means of possessing the empire
without any more fears; it also explains both the conquest of
Melos and the expedition against Sicily. The second attitude
is firmly defended by Cleon when Mytilene has revolted, and
it can be detected in the anger and sternness of Athens during
Brasidas's campaign.

But it is obvious that such a need to increase, over and
over, one's own power involves a danger which itself becomes
greater and greater, as each remedy but adds to the number
of potential or actual enemies. This consequence is not at all
so clear in Thucydides as is the progress of imperialism. It is
never put forward in so many words. Yet it emerges whenever
Athens is shown to act against prudence (when Pericles says

he fears Athens's mistakes more than anything else; when she refuses the offer of peace at the time of Pylos; when she adopts cruel decisions toward cities, after having seen in the case of Mytilene that this was wrong; when she starts new conquests, particularly in Sicily). But it shows also in a brief remark, made more important by its position in the work. In the dialogue of Melos, just before the Sicilian expedition, the Melians ask how it can be possible that the policy of Athens should not increase the number of her foes (v. 98)—a question to which the Athenians don't give an answer. The danger is therefore clearly apparent in the work. I should say it inspires Thucydides' remark in II. 65. 11, when he speaks of the many mistakes made by Athens "as happens for a great city owning an empire."

Power, therefore, leads to increase in power, not because it is an easy temptation, as in the simple pattern we started from, but because a powerful state has to act that way. As things go on, the path of prudence gets narrower and narrower: *hybris* and its dangers are rooted in the very nature of power.

Such a diagnosis is a discovery, and a terrifying one. But Thucydides goes even further, for he doesn't satisfy himself after he has brought to light that necessity of action and that increasing risk of mistakes. He also explains how and why these mistakes are actually made. This, I think, will be our surprise. The problem is stated in political terms and is marked by lucidity and realism; but the reasons for the mistakes, the reasons for the wrong choice of policy, are ultimately moral reasons. Thucydides undoubtedly turns our attention in that direction. This is not to say that he ever dwells on morality as such, nor even in its simple relation to *hybris*. He doesn't. But what he offers us is an analysis of the mechanism by which political mistakes arise from a decline in civic morality. He has not only described the new form of *hybris* and connected it with the very nature of power; he has let his readers see how it works by a thorough and coherent analysis of political psychology.

Of the three ways in which politics are affected by a decline in civic morality, the first is the most obvious. It concerns the morality of the orators and politicians.

The question of their morality is clearly brought forth by Thucydides in his judgment on Pericles in II. 65. There, he explains that the war could have been a success if Athens had kept to Periclean policy and had committed no imprudent act. Now his successors were, in fact, imprudent and their enterprises brought harm to the city because they acted "according to private ambition and for private gain," that is to say because they "looked for their own honor and advantage" (7). Pericles never indulged the people's pleasure (8: πρὸς ἡδονὴν): he could oppose both the confidence of *hybris* (9) and any unreasonable fright. But his successors, being practically equal to each other and "aiming, each for his own part, at the first position in the state, let the pleasure of the people take command of the city's policy. Hence so many mistakes . . ." (10–11). The explanation is quite clear: it points to a decline in the civic morality of the leaders, who resort to flattery.

This, it may be added, finds a sort of complement in the analysis of both Cleon and Diodotus discussing the treatment of Mytilene: the former accuses the orators of aiming at nothing but rhetorical success or personal profit (III. 38); the latter shows that all such insinuations, and the more so when they are made for money, frighten away the wise orator and thus bring harm to the city (III. 42). Between them, Cleon and Diodotus confirm the explanation given in II. 65.

Dishonest advice may be used for all sorts of policies. We have mentioned flattery, and it seems that the general theme of flattery—which plays such an important part in all the attacks against the demagogues—is not foreign to the notions of *hybris* and imprudence. Flattery doesn't consist only in telling the people, directly, that they are admired and admirable —as Aristophanes mockingly presents it, speaking of the pleasure the people receive when hearing about Athens "crowned with violets" or "brilliant" (*Ach.* 637–40). Flattery often consisted in telling the people they could get even larger and

broader power, producing advantages and salaries; that is what
Cleon and his rival both do in the *Knights*. Cleon indeed is
made to say that his purpose is that Demos should "command
over all Greeks" (797).

In other words, the state acts like an individual, listening
to his pleasures and passions instead of listening to the voice
of reason and prudence or, as the Greeks used to say, instead
of considering "what is best." But the voice of prudence and
reason can only be represented by an honest and lucid orator.
The people are easy to deceive, prompt to enthusiasm or de-
spondency, full of passions, ready for *hybris*: if the orators are
not honest or lucid enough to say "what is best," the mistakes
cannot be avoided. Pericles represented the state's reason;
Cleon and Alcibiades act according to the people's pleasure,
which Plato would call its ἐπιθυμίαι.[11]

Now it is a fact that this notion, so clearly formulated by
Thucydides, has inspired the philosophers and orators of the
following century and the reactions of people like Plato or
Isocrates and Demosthenes. It led Plato to try to rebuild a
city obeying justice and reason. It led Isocrates and other
orators to try to reform Athens by reforming her civic morality.

Isocrates insisted mainly on the moral influence the Areo-
pagus could have. His great concern was that Athens should
get rid of "those who please you on the moment, but do not
care about the future, and pretend to love the people, but
ruin the whole state" (*Peace* 121). As he says, "it is of far
greater opportunity to practice virtue and to fight down vices
for a city than for an individual; for an impious or bad man may
die before he has to pay for his faults, whereas a city, being
immortal, is always there to be punished both by men and
by the gods" (119–20).

As for these orators who spoke to please the people, πρὸς
χάριν or πρὸς ἡδονὴν, instead of seeking "what is best," who
indeed ever blamed them for causing the ruin of the city more
than Demosthenes? Who complained, more than he did, of the
irresponsibility of the people in leaving the way open to orators
who were traitors? After all, his great pride consists in the

fact that "being as able as others to accuse, and flatter, and confiscate, as they do, [he] has never obeyed such maxims or been led by either gain or ambition [οὔθ᾽ ὑπὸ κέρδους οὔθ᾽ ὑπὸ φιλοτιμίας]: he has kept saying what should mean, for himself, an inferior credit in Athens, but, for Athens, a greater one." He even concludes this very passage by a reflection which could be a paraphrase of Thucydides, saying: "Toward the easiest things, nature will go by itself; as for the best, it needs a lesson, taught in his speeches by the good citizen" (*Chers.* 71–72).

But these very similarities must not deceive us. Demosthenes, no doubt, fights the same evil as Thucydides, but not in relation to political *hybris* as the historian did. In a way, the parallel would be more significant with a period and a state in which the passion of the multitude was similarly fought by a rational instance. I am here thinking—and that is one example among many which could be given—of the passage where Plutarch tells us about Nasica's refusal to allow Carthage to be destroyed: he writes that Nasica "saw the people already misbehaving through *hybris*, and saw that prosperity and pride were making this people hard to lead for the Senate, so that it had in fact the power of taking the whole state by force along the path of its own desires" (*Cato* 27. 3: ὁρμαῖς).[12] The multitude does not overcome the orator, but the Senate; and it is not because the right influence is missing, but because it is to no avail. On the whole, however, the explanation of mistakes and disorders is the same.

That Thucydides should have so clearly denounced this cause for mistakes is, no doubt, to his merit. That he should have inserted the analysis of internal policy in the whole problem of power makes this merit far greater. Still, it leaves us with an explanation which is not wholly satisfactory, because it doesn't get to the bottom of the question—a reproach which is seldom appropriate with Thucydides. Why did it happen that the leaders who followed Pericles lacked civic morality?—perhaps because such a disposition is the usual attitude of mankind and Pericles was only an exception. But

one circumstance should call our attention to another possibility which may have greatly added to this natural disposition.

When Cleon complained of the ways the orators behaved,
he was accusing the people: "You are responsible for it, you
bad organizers of the competition, for you are in the habit
of contemplating words and listening to actions. . . ."[13] The
same trend of reproach is to be found in Isocrates and Demosthenes; when they complained about the behavior of the
orators, they also made the people responsible for it. Both
of them keep trying to stir the people's virtue or patriotism.
Both of them also keep contrasting the merits of yore to the
present folly or lethargy. Now this leads us to another aspect
of the decline in civic morality concerning, this time, not the
orators but the people.

Did Thucydides ever suggest such a cause for the mistakes
made by Athens? At first sight, we might doubt it, for, if
he does speak of a decline in public morality as a general result
of the war, he never says it had some bearing on Athenian
policy. Yet, it may be worthwhile considering a little more
closely the two famous passages where he describes it.

The first one is the analysis of the moral consequences of
the plague; the second one is the analysis of the moral consequences of civil war, which is itself an indirect consequence
of the war. These are two long passages, the presence of which
is already remarkable in our realistic historian.

Indeed, why does he insist so much on such ideas? In
the case of the plague, no political intention emerges; but still,
we may notice that Thucydides presents this moral perturba-
tion as the beginning of a more general evolution in public
morality; and he does it with great emphasis: πρῶτόν τε
ἦρξε καὶ ἐς τἆλλα τῇ πόλει ἐπὶ πλέον ἀνομίας (emphasis mine
[II. 53. 1]). All words point to an evolution that will be continued. We have more in the second passage, the point of
which is, this time, very clear. The text is not an excursus
or a general reflection about war in general; it has a precise

function which emerges as soon as the passage is brought in relation with others.

A decline in morality is shown in III. 82, and the cause of this decline, says Thucydides, is "power pursued for the sake of greed and ambition (8: διὰ πλεονεξίαν καὶ φιλοτιμίαν).[14] These two feelings produce rivalry and contention (φιλονικεῖν, φιλονικίαν). Now, this analysis and these very words record what we have seen in II. 65. The feelings are the same, and we now discover that the evil which marred the orators' attitude was indeed a general evil. If the orators acted κατὰ τὰς ἰδίας φιλοτιμίας καὶ ἴδια κέρδη (II. 65. 7), this was because they partook in an evolution which touched even the people in all the cities of Greece.[15] This evolution thus explains, in an indirect manner, the final fall of Athens.

Perhaps the two passages were not written at the same time. Certainly III. 82 doesn't hint, even in the faintest fashion, at the downfall of Athens. But the interest is precisely directed toward the very evil which was to prove so disastrous.

Also, the whole passage is a condemnation of *stasis* and shows its dangers. While reading it, it would be most difficult not to bear in mind that this *stasis*, that had caused so many calamities in Greece, was finally to reach Athens herself, in 411 and 404 B.C. A great part of Book VIII is a description of *stasis*. Once more, in II. 65, this evil is given pride of place among the causes of the defeat of Athens. She was ruined, as it says, because of her divisions, and the Athenians fell κατὰ τὰς ἰδίας διαφοράς.

This judgment is undoubtedly justified, for the Athenians as early as 411 B.C. were turning their attention and courage toward their internal strife. Once it required all the firmness of the proponents of concord, or *homonoia*, to prevent a real slaughter in Samos—they had to remind the people that the enemy's fleet was stationed just in front (VIII. 75. 1). Another time, Alcibiades stopped the army from leaving Samos altogether to sail against Athens. Thucydides, mentioning the fact, adds a comment of his own: "that would obviously give the Ionian region and the Hellespont to the enemy"

(VIII. 86. 4). Even if that danger were averted, it is certain that *stasis*, which was the result of a crisis in civic morality, harmed Athens in 411 B.C. as it was to harm her again in 404 B.C. If III. 82 was written before these two episodes, it means Thucydides could already measure the importance of the evil. Indeed, neither the orators nor the people in general were considering the interest of the state before their own any more. This was a result of the hardships of the war, which itself was a result of a policy of conquest and power.

Now, with these two notions (φιλοτιμία–πλεονεξία on the one hand, *stasis* on the other), we have the starting point of a whole series of texts and reflections which fill both Greek and Latin literatures. *Pleonexia* and *philotimia*, from Thucydides onward, form a pair forever after. They recur in many authors, for example in the *Catiline*, when Sallust denounces "pecuniae, deinde imperi cupido" or, with varied vocabulary, "avaritia et ambitio" (10. 3–4). They also recur in all the authors who dwell on Rome's moral decline.[16] As for *stasis*, as well as concord, its opposite, its importance emerges both in Isocrates and Plato.[17] It never disappeared from Greek or Latin reflection about the fall of nations: *concordia* was, of course, of primary importance to Sallust; and Montesquieu, in *Considérations sur les causes de la grandeur des Romains et de leur décadence*, gives "Des divisions qui furent toujours dans la ville" as title to his chapter 8.[18]

The so-called realism, which is so much insisted upon as soon as Thucydides is mentioned, has often blinded us to this remarkable insistence on civic morality. It is often said that Thucydides leaves aside all considerations of morality.[19] I think it was well worth observing the important part he really has in launching all classical reflection in that direction.

Perhaps even that doesn't do justice to the moral analysis he offers us in relation to the rise and fall of Athens. Before leaving him, I would like to add that this moral decline shows in his work in still another manner which is both important and relevant to our theme: it is the idea that the people gradually lost not only their civic morality but their ideal and the faith they had formerly placed in their own greatness.

Thucydides doesn't say this any more than he actually formulated the last idea we examined. But I think it may be inferred, with enough safety, from the way he describes Athens's policy. First of all, there is the Funeral Speech, the Epitaphios. It does exist in the work, and it is very far from only grouping a series of clichés such as those usually found in this kind of speech. It insists, not on Athens's great deeds, but on her virtues and her glory. It shows that her power rests on a sense of freedom and generosity. It says that no subject could protest that he is governed by people who are unworthy of governing and it asks the Athenians to stay in love with the city's power and to keep giving their lives willingly for its glory. Now the same idealism appears in some parts of Pericles' last speech, but nowhere else in the work, or nowhere else at all. Both the presence of such a speech and the absence of any similar echo in the following parts of Thucydides' *History* do stir our attention—or should do so.

It is not only a presence against an absence; I think we can follow, in the speeches made by Athenian speakers in Thucydides, a sort of regular decline in idealism accompanied by a progress of greed and by a more and more realistic emphasis on power as such. The Athenians of Book I dwell on the memory of the Persian Wars (I. 74), which made them worthy of respect.[20] The Athenians of Book v cancel the idea as a vain topic (v. 89). Euphemos in Book VI mentions it again, but with an addition that is a strong correction: "We rule over others, being worthy of it, and also because we yearned for some strength which we could use against the Peloponnese" (VI. 83. 1). The same evolution shows for the argument of practical interest (*xumpheron*), which tends to eliminate all others. The Athenians in Book I mention practical advantage (*ôphelia*) along with two other feelings, one of which is glory (*timê*); if they obeyed *to xumpheron*, they say it is an admitted behavior in the case of great dangers.[21] But the Athenians in Melos begin with the affirmation that they won't accept any

other kind of argument (v. 89–90); Euphemos, in Camarina,
insists throughout on security and interest, saying that for a
city having an empire, nothing is illogical that is *xumpheron*
(vi. 85. 1)[22] The political condition of power, which was mentioned at the very beginning of our description of Thucydides'
thought on the rise and fall of Athens, seems, therefore, to be
more and more easily admitted.

After all, it is a fact that, as the war went on, Athens's
tyranny grew more and more oppressive. The Athenians were
angered by defections, irritated by war, dispirited by suffering;
the teaching of the sophists lent its dialectic skepticism to their
new feelings. Repressions became more severe as can be seen
in the case of Torone, Skione, and Melos, coming after Mytilene.[23] Conquest became either quite unjustified (as in the
case of Melos) or of immense scope (as in the case of Sicily).
Shall we be asked to believe that this obvious hardening in
the justifications Thucydides lends his Athenian orators and
the obvious hardening of Athens's actual policy are a mere
coincidence? That would be asking a great deal.[24]

This hardening exists, and it shows in Thucydides. It
means that we can read in his work not only the transformation
of a policy, but the progressive decay of its inner supports
—this love of honor, of justice, of action, of glory, and this
readiness to give everything for their sake, which had been
so brilliantly celebrated by Pericles. I think we should pay
attention to the fact that twice in his work Thucydides goes
out of his way to dwell on the moral implications of Athenian
power; he does so in the Funeral Speech, with all its high-minded
idealism; and he does so in the dialogue of Melos, with all its
crude and harsh realism. The very existence of these two texts
is singular; the place chosen for the second one is not less
remarkable. This dialogue, which is the only one in the work
and is also the only one where the danger of increasing the
number of one's enemies is mentioned, takes place on the very
occasion where both conquest and repression are at their peak
and on the eve of the Sicilian expedition, which will be the
turning point of the whole war—the moment when political

hybris, now at its height, opens the way to the beginning of political *nemesis.*

Thucydides' realism ultimately consists, then, in showing that what counts more than anything in the preservation of power is morality—both for the individuals and for the state, both in particular decisions and in the deepest aspirations of the citizens as such.

Indeed, Thucydides almost gives us a complete analysis of moral decline as a cause for the ruin of states. If I say "almost," it is that before we finish with *hybris,* we must be aware it can develop in quite a different manner. In Thucydides, it led the people, through exasperation, to become harder and more imprudent. Later, it was also seen to breed self-complacency and to leave the people lazy, devoid of courage or ambition. Thus we have an evolution which in a way is contrary to ordinary *hybris* for it works in the opposite way, but which finally comes to the same conclusion as it explains the passage from power to downfall by the corrupting influence of security, prosperity, and power.

In the fourth century B.C., both trends seem to mingle in Isocrates or to appear alternately. In his treatise *On the Peace,* he denounces the greed and folly of Athens and the dangers of dominion as such; his inspiration is there obviously derived from Thucydides. But in his other works, although he speaks for hegemony and not for dominion, he keeps returning with passion and obstinacy to the memory of the Persian Wars and to the generous ideas of the past. He wants, according to occasion and circumstances, to restrain the city's ambition or stir up her dynamism.[25]

In Demosthenes, the second attitude is the only one to be found. In every single speech he gives, he tries in vain to stir up his city, to remind her of the Persian Wars, that is to say of her former glory and generosity.[26] He takes after Pericles, and he wants to restrain a dangerous disposition leading his fellow citizens not to over-ambitious conquest, but to indifference.

In later times, when the example of Rome offered to the attention of historians the image of a city that could experience moral decline without being directly threatened by enemies and war, it soon emerged that the two factors which had ruined Athens's policy by inspiring her rash and irresponsible enterprises could also threaten the Roman Empire from within by sheer internal decay and lack of spirit. New themes were then added to Thucydides' description, so as to fit the new experience: slight changes, some new words, and the ancient pattern was thus made to express a new reality.

Thucydides had mentioned greed as an element of civil strife, but he could not speak of luxury, for in the case of Athens and her continued war, no evolution of that kind had occurred. The arrival of wealth, however, was one of the causes which ruined Sparta, and it certainly modified the attitude of the Romans. This offered still another pattern of *hybris*, based on private luxury—being rich leads to indolence, idleness, and insubordination—which, of course, spoils both political energy and military efficiency. Once more, some form of excess leads to downfall.

This function of private luxury should demand attention, for it shows the difference between the Greek approach and our modern views. What we should call this "private luxury" would be "economic crisis." The increase of wealth didn't extend equally to all citizens any more than economic difficulties had been similar for all during the Peloponnesian War. We should here make a distinction between classes. What the Greeks saw was the city as a whole and its moral transformation. Strangely enough, these two different languages do express the same thing.

This pattern of *hybris* shows, however, in Polybius. We shall be dealing with him more at length in the following chapter but it should be noted that he clearly had such an idea. It appears, for instance, in vi. 57 where he says: "When a state has escaped many serious dangers and achieved an unquestioned supremacy and dominion, it is clear that, with prosperity growing within, life becomes more luxurious and men

more tense in rivalry about their public ambitions and enterprises." Speaking of the Roman decline in political morality
is indeed a habit among all authors. Some of them place its
beginning in 200 B.C., others in 168 B.C., others in 146 B.C., but
all agree that such a decline took place after Rome had become
powerful. Polybius worries at the change in morality which
he actually observes (XVIII. 35; XXXI. 25); Livy deplores the
fact that Rome is already in some sort of crisis coming from
her greatness and says the city suffers from this greatness
(Preface, 4: "cum jam magnitudine laboret sua"). Sallust insists on this evolution.[27] Cicero acknowledges it also (*De Rep.*
v. 1) and Florus, as I have quoted him before, also speaks of
Rome rising so high that she labored under her own power
(III. 12: "eo magnitudine crescere ut viribus suis conficeretur").
He indeed accused "nimia felicitas." Why not?—everyone did,
and this was to remain. Montesquieu repeated the idea with still
more insistence on luxury: "La grandeur de l'État fit la grandeur des fortunes particulières. Mais, comme l'opulence est dans
les mœurs, et non pas dans les richesses, celles des Romains,
qui ne laissaient pas d'avoir des bornes, produisirent un luxe
et des profusions qui n'en avaient pas."[28] Gibbon also insists
on the fact that the Romans had learned military virtues
through poverty, but soon lost their discipline and civism in
three centuries of apparent prosperity (VII). He gives a similar
description, only more schematic, of the luxury which marked
the decline of the power the Saracens had acquired while dis-
regarding such riches (52). Indeed, I am not sure that the
very notion of "decline and fall," which has come to replace
"rise and fall," does not always convey, in a more or less implicit way, this notion that power creates a decline in morality,
which itself produces the loss of this former power.[29]

In all these cases, we find the last form of the old *hybris-
nemesis* pattern, founded on the psychology of peoples. That
this new basis started in a very thorough analysis of Thucydides, I hope I have made clear. But what we find at the
end of this long line of authors is fairly different from what
we had at the start. The difference, as has been already sug-

gested, is partly due to circumstances. This explains not only the new importance of luxury or the like, but the fact that Athens had known a life of restless and unsteady dominion, whereas Rome experienced the danger of having no more enemies to be afraid of: this spoils first the military training which helps, in a practical way, the acquisition of power,[30] but it also spoils the zeal and ardor of the people. Now, this value of the *metus hostilis* is, practically speaking, a Roman theme.[31] Political theory, indeed, always develops in close connection with political events and conforms to actuality.

The difference, however, is not only one of circumstances. All the moral analysis in Thucydides is part of a large system which is as precise and complex as the mechanism of a clock. In his work, the whole fact of moral decline, with all its different aspects carefully distinguished and described, enters the picture only as a cause for mistakes in a situation previously existing, which, by itself, makes it necessary for a state to go on rising once it has begun to and makes it more and more difficult for it to avoid the mistakes which may cause it to fall. Moral decline explains the mistakes, but the political condition of power explains both the possibility of this decline and the particular danger it involves. The diagnosis is thus precise and complete. The authors who followed Thucydides and borrowed either one theme or another from him never reached the same acuteness in combining them all with a theory of power.

Precisely because it rested on such a thorough view of the rise and fall of Athens, Thucydides' analysis leaves his reader with an *aporia*. As he describes them, the ways of political wisdom are extremely difficult; the problem is almost impossible to solve. Once given the original condition of power as a tyranny, which he has so magnificently described, how could one succeed? How could one rise and not fall? How can one avoid the different forms of *hybris* connected with power or the various forms of psychological influence which develop as the inner accompaniment of power? Is it even possible? Can one try to organize power on another basis that would make avoiding mistakes a less difficult task? That is a problem Thucydides didn't deal with, and that is exactly where he left us. By a remarkable circumstance, that is also exactly where his followers took up the problem. Political theory conforms to actual events, but it also has its continuity and coherence.

Indeed, if you couldn't maintain an empire built on fear and hatred, you had to use your strength and means in some other way to try to build up something different. This was the great problem for the authors who followed; it will also be the theme of chapter IV.

IV

The Organization of Power

The lesson arising from Athenian experience in the fifth century B.C. had been a severe one. But we should not forget — although Thucydides doesn't insist on its nature and principles—that, in front of Athens, there stood another powerful city that had been powerful for quite a long time and whose power was very different from that of Athens—namely, Sparta.

Sparta had no sea power, no treasury. She had command over cities that had an equal right in all decisions and didn't hate her.[1] Once her league in the Peloponnese was organized, she didn't attempt any new conquest for more than a century; she wasn't, therefore, an object of fear. She had indeed organized her own dominion in such a way that the political condition Thucydides describes as prevailing for Athens didn't exist or interfere in her case. The lesson could then have been to follow her example—had she not disregarded it herself. However, at the end of the Peloponnesian War, having acquired a navy in order to fight Athens and having used Persian money in order to achieve victory, she immediately changed her style once she was victorious. She turned into a domineering nation and was soon both feared and hated—till she finally collapsed in her turn. She collapsed under Theban pressure soon after she had taken possession of the acropolis of Thebes, causing a great scandal throughout all Greece—so much so that her faithful admirer, Xenophon, goes out of his way in the *Hellenics* to speak, for that occasion, of the hand of God punishing the wrongdoers.[2]

63

This was probably one of the reasons why, in the fourth century, B.C., even those who turned to Sparta for a model of internal constitution never turned to her for a model of external policy.³ On the contrary, the lesson arising from the Athenian experience seemed to find in the Spartan experience a confirmation, making it more obvious and more decisive. This, in any case, is the light in which Isocrates sees it; he insists, in his treatise *On the Peace*, on this revealing parallelism.

The problem, therefore, remained in all its urgency. Political leaders had to try to invent a means of achieving power and influence for their city without ending in a tyranny like that of Athens, with the unavoidable doom that would involve. Political thinkers had to find theories in order to forestall such a policy or to describe it in a useful manner. Thus, we shall find new political notions which in the fourth century B.C. centered on Greece and in the second century B.C., on Rome.

Isocrates is the main representative of the first group. His attitude toward Athenian policy and power is, in fact, illuminating. He seems to be always changing his mind, though he never did. Having read his Thucydides, he was possessed by the wish to help restore the glamour of Athens's greatness as she had known it from the time of the Persian Wars till the time of Pericles; but he was seized with horror at the idea she could once more undergo the same evolution. I hope this sentimental description is not untrue to his obstinacy.

Indeed, his first attempt was the *Panegyric* in which he vindicates hegemony for Athens, extolls her merits, and praises her past dominion. He insists, however, that she should beware of turning that hegemony into an empire which would be hated. Then the second confederation was founded, according to his wishes and in agreement with his suggestions, for it was to have no tribute and no encroachment on the autonomy of the cities. But Athens soon found herself fighting the so-called Social War, that is to say fighting some of the allies she was supposed to treat with such equity. Isocrates, admitting it was her own fault,[4] wrote his treatise *On the Peace*, which deals severely with the excesses and imprudence of Athens's past dominion. Then, not resigning from his general ideal, he turns to other possible leaders of Greece and gives them advice. When Philip appears on the stage of Greek politics, Isocrates advises Philip to make good use of the hegemony he will acquire in Greece and to beware of becoming unpopular. Isocrates also returns to the idea that Athens could again have her chance, headed by Philip, and that the great hope of the *Panegyric* may, in some way, be partly recovered: this is the idea which inspires the *Panathenaic*.

This oscillating movement between praise and condemnation has its source in a very clear idea of how power should be organized in order to endure and to be accepted: two notions give the key to his program—namely, *eunoia* ("goodwill") and *homonoia* ("concord").

Eunoia is exactly what Thucydides had shown the Athenian Empire to have destroyed, and missed.[5] Instead of *eunoia* producing trust, say the Mytilenians, the Athenian Empire rests on fear (III. 12. 1). Diodotus regrets that the Athenians don't try, by tolerance, to keep whatever slight *eunoia* remains for them among their subjects (III. 47. 2). On the other hand, Brasidas tries to make good use of the cities' *eunoia* toward Sparta (IV. 87. 3; 114. 4); everyone knows how dangerous that effort proves for Athens. In fact, throughout all Greece, Athens can reckon with no *eunoia*: the *eunoia* of Greece is largely in favor of Sparta, as Thucydides tells his reader at the very start (II. 8. 4).

This is why the aim could seem to be to reconcile power and *eunoia*. In Thucydides, this possibility was mentioned but once, as a hope for Sparta in case she were victorious (VI. 92. 5: τῆς ἁπάσης ʽΕλλάδος ἑκούσης καὶ οὐ βίᾳ, κατ᾽ εὔνοιαν δὲ ἡγῆσθε).

Now, for Isocrates, this notion is central and is particularly evident in the treatise *On the Peace*, where he constructs the whole dialectic of rise and fall around a pair of contrasting terms: *eunoia–misos* ("goodwill"–"hatred").[6] But how, and by what policy, can one escape *misos* and gather *eunoia*, while being powerful? What is Athens to do? What are states to do? Isocrates knows two ways: one negative, the other positive.

The negative way is to avoid the mistakes of the Athenian Empire and to refrain from doing any of the things which are hateful to cities because they are a limitation to autonomy. He had hinted in the *Panegyric* at the remedy a single decree could bring (114). This was no doubt a preparation to what Aristoteles' decree was to be three years later, when the second confederation was founded. The general idea is again summed up in the treatise *On the Peace*, when he indicates the various means of restoring and improving the situation of the state. The first is to change advisers. The second condition to create change is more precise: things would be right, he says, "if we accepted treating our allies as friends, instead of leaving them autonomous on principle, but abandoning them in reality to the *strategoi* and to any treatment these *strategoi* decide, if we command over them not as masters, but as allies" (133).

This means Isocrates is the first to discover the virtues of being fair and moderate to people. Indeed, the very vocabulary reflects this new trend. Whereas πρᾶος ("kind") is attested to only three times in Herodotus and once in Thucydides, Isocrates presents thirty-one instances of the word. Whereas ἐπιεικής ("fair, moderate") is attested to only four times in Herodotus and nine times in Thucydides, Isocrates presents not less than forty-two examples of the word. No doubt they do not all apply to the idea we are now examining, but a great many examples do; no other author presents such a frequent use of the word. This progress in the use of the word is the sign of a new value and policy. It recommends a new attitude toward people.

That may seem a fairly simple and naive program. Yet, one should not consider it with contempt, for Isocrates, with this moral predication, was in fact laying the principles which were to allow for federations and confederations, that is to say associations of cities keeping their autonomy and observing some rules. Not only the league of Corinth was to follow his principles, but also all the attempted or successful leagues which developed in the fourth century B.C. and paved the way for the great Hellenistic leagues, whether Achaean, Aetolian, or otherwise. This was opening a new perspective for Greek power policy. I should beware of forgetting that notion especially in the huge and powerful country called the "United States of America"!

This was not all, however, for the great means Isocrates saw for acquiring *eunoia* was more positive. With the model of the first Confederation at its start, Isocrates perceived that *eunoia* was indeed acquired by the state holding a generous and active policy, helping others, being admired by them, and being therefore considered worthy of supremacy.

This idea of being worthy of supremacy was not new. It is found in Herodotus and Thucydides,[7] where Athens's action during the Persian War proved helpful to all Greeks and made her worthy of being their leader. Isocrates, however, turned the idea into a general theory. He endeavored to show that Athens deserved leadership in Greece because of the many services she did for her (*Paneg.* 22); he insisted that she was "worthy of the greatest praise" (75), that her behavior was "worthy of hegemony" (98). Such behavior produces spontaneous *eunoia*. It did after the Persian War. It will if anyone acts in a similar way. Later Isocrates advised Philip to undertake a policy which would be supported by the Greek *eunoia*.

This means that a powerful state must not only beware not to encroach on the cities' autonomy, but also must, before that, always choose and follow a policy that will be both active and generous, so that the cities will benefit from it and approve or admire it.

This leads us to the second catchword of Isocrates' program, that is to say *homonoia*, or concord. Concord within the state is one thing—and an important condition for the rise or preservation of that state. Isocrates didn't ignore it, he even insisted on the idea. But he saw further and was the first to insist on the importance of concord between the different states as a means of stability for the power of the group they form and for the power of their leader. If the leading state chooses a policy which all the others approve of, there will be concord. The *eunoia* of all is, indeed, concord.

But what policy could produce such a result in Greece, if not the policy consisting in the defense of the Greeks in general? A successful leadership in Greece could only exist with a Panhellenic program. The importance of that idea in Isocrates is well known: it is the basis of everything he ever thought or wrote.

The result is that an empire resting on force will be replaced, not only by a league, but by a new political unit resting on common traditions and joined in common action against common enemies. Isocrates saw it quite clearly: "It is impossible to have a lasting peace without making a common war against the barbarians, and impossible to have concord in Greece before we have shared advantages having one and the same origin, and shared dangers against one and the same enemy" (*Paneg.* 173).

By his negative advice, Isocrates was paving the way for federations; by his positive advice, he was laying the foundations of Panhellenic power and of Greece considered as a living reality.

The rise and preservation of a state is then only possible, in Isocrates' opinion, if what it creates, leads, and promotes is not its own power, but the power of a collection of states united in a common action and ideal. That it failed to happen may not surprise us. It is not easy to change prospects in such a way. The feeling of independence, in Greek cities, made them touchy: a great power was needed to impose the new ideal, and a great power was likely to overlook it. Indeed, after Athens, though apparently following Isocrates' negative advice, had disappointed him and proved incapable of realizing the positive program, Philip and Alexander did realize some of his views, but both treated Greece and the Greek cities without the kindness and moderation he had wished. Moreover, the great enterprises of the latter soon exceeded the range of Panhellenism.

Yet, in a rather idealistic and utopian way, Isocrates' scheme for ensuring a lasting supremacy and organizing an accepted power could be said to prepare what another state was to do with success and what later writers were to describe with surprise and wonder.

In the second century B.C. this state, of course, was Rome. Polybius's aim was to explain how and with what *politeia* Rome attained sovereignty extending to the whole world. It is easy to see that, in many ways, his description takes after the analyses of both Thucydides and Isocrates (whether he knew them or not by direct information); but the reality he was describing and the events he had experienced could not but show in his work: they enable us to perceive a new approach to the old problem of organizing power.

In the first instance, he understood, after Thucydides and Isocrates, that the main task for a state is not to rise but to endure and that it is difficult, in prosperity, not to undergo such changes as might endanger what one has conquered. We have already mentioned his condemnation of private luxury as a result of conquest. But we can trace in his work a more precise idea of what one must be careful to do or not to do.

First, one must beware of any change in one's habits. This indeed is a defense of morality, civism, valiance, and austerity: such are the virtues which allow a state to rise. To abandon these virtues is wrong, and Polybius first condemns such an attitude by an a priori argument. He does that for the two main states he is dealing with, Carthage and Rome; the following two passages reveal this trend of thought.

In Book IX. 10, he speaks about the Romans' spoliations and their seizure of works of art, saying: "If it had been by such means that they had brought out the rise of their country, no doubt they were right in bringing back home the kind of things wich had contributed to their increase. But if they had led the most simple life and kept as far as possible from any excess or luxury of that kind, and still succeeded in dominating the people who had the most numerous and beautiful treasuries of that sort, how could one refuse the conclusion that what they did was a mistake?" For Polybius, the Romans then changed the ἔθη of the victorious party for those of the defeated one. Art and luxury took the place of austerity and valiance. This was an obvious drawback.

Similarly, in Book x. 36, he mentions the folly of the Carthaginians. When they had destroyed the Roman armies in Spain, they treated their Spanish allies with arrogance: "they thought that there is one way for reaching power and another one for keeping it; they didn't understand that the best manner of preserving superiority is to cling, as well as one can, to the moral attitudes with which one has acquired this superiority." Indeed, the Carthaginians, according to the old *hybris* pattern, were then elated by success, and they believed they could rely on it forever (ὑπολαβόντες ἀδήριτον αὐτοῖς ὑπάρχειν τὴν Ἰβηρίαν). Polybius condemns *hybris* by a logical argument based on practical opportunity.

This logical condemnation of *hybris* was to remain a classical topic of political reflection. As Sallust writes in the *Catiline* (2. 5): "Power is easily preserved by the same qualities which it was first obtained with; but when idleness seizes the place of toil, passion and arrogance the place of self-control and equity, then fortune undergoes the same change as do the habits of life (*moribus*)."[8]

But if we look a little more closely at this change of habits that Polybius condemns and at its danger, we are soon brought back to the very analysis of our two previous authors. Indeed, in the two passages I have just quoted, there is a precise comment declaring that what was wrong in the Carthaginian and Roman attitudes was that it deprived them of the *eunoia* of people—this *eunoia* which is the condition and basis of any lasting power.

In Book ix. 10, he explains that the works of art stolen and exhibited by the Romans stir up hostility among those who see them. His analysis is quite insistent: whereas the idea of not changing one's ἔθη takes ten lines, the ideas of jealousy and hatred (φθόνος and μῖσος) take eighteen, and the passage ends in general advice to all those who may attempt to rise to power. These exhibitions, he says, inspire envy, which "is the worst thing that people superior in power have to fear." This envy increases as the victorious city goes on following the same way. Then wrath is added to envy and this produces hatred. Isocrates wouldn't have used different language.[9]

The same insistence on a general lesson is equally remarkable in the passage dealing with the Carthaginians. Polybius says that such an evolution has taken place quite often (πλεονάκις) and that one could find quite a number of people (πολλαπλασίους) who made the same mistake, for it has been seen in many instances (ἐπὶ πολλῶν ἤδη). Indeed, "it requires more experience to make good use of success than to achieve it," and "men achieve success by behaving well to people and offering good hope to their neighbors, but, when they have reached what they wanted, they behave badly and command as masters to their subjects, so that, as one could expect, the change in the leading people is accompanied by an equal change in the subjects' attitude." The result is, in the present case, that these subjects take the first opportunity to abandon Hasdrubal and the Carthaginian party. This, again, could be written by Isocrates.

Just as Isocrates had advocated the pursuit of goodwill (or *eunoia*) by a fair and moderate attitude (*epieikes*), Polybius insists all through his work on the dangers of roughness or severity and on the advantages of kindness, which procures *eunoia*. The vocabulary, however, has changed; *epieikeia*, which was still very close to righteousness, is often replaced by a new word, deliberately different and requiring more than justice, namely, benevolence or *philanthropia*. This may be what the Romans called their *clementia*, only it has the Greek generality and a wider range. Also, it applies to all people and conditions; many are the examples of good or bad policy which come from all sides to illustrate the idea.

How does one rise? Apparently, by being nice to people and by winning their sympathy. This notion, which may sound childish, shows in the case of several individuals, who are treated as a series of models for good or bad conduct. The elder Tarquin became a king because he behaved so well that he was trusted, considered with gratitude and with *eunoia* (vi. 11a: εὔνοιαν).[10]

Philip the second, who seems to be a sort of monster when we read Demosthenes, is said to have achieved less by his victories than by his clemency and humanity. No doubt the boldness of such a statement implies great conviction on the part of the author.[11] In fact, all the words meaning clemency and a conduct worthy of *eunoia* are added to one another (v. 10: ἐπιεικείας καὶ φιλανθρωπίας εὐγνωμοσύνῃ καὶ μετριότητι, πρᾳότητος καὶ καλοκἀγαθίας). Polybius even draws a firm conclusion: "Through his shrewdness he produced at small cost a great result; and the spirit of the Athenians was so much struck by his generosity that, having been his foes, they became his ready allies."

Now the other Philip, who belongs to Polybius's history and is therefore treated directly, began in the same way. He began amidst goodwill and zeal (vii. 11: ταῖς εὐνοίαις - εὐνοίας καὶ προθυμίας). The result is that nobody revolts, nobody attacks him, all are eager to help; people love him for his "good deeds" (εὐεργετικόν). Then he changed and chose the opposite attitude: as could be expected, he thus "caused a change for the reverse both in the people's feeling toward him and in the very success of his own action."

Now, that is exactly the way people do fall. Scopas, the Aetolian commander, has unlimited greed (xiii. 2. 5: ἀπληστίαν); this causes envy, and he loses both his fortune and his life.[12]

The same optimistic theory also pertains in the case of powerful states. For them also Polybius is careful to dwell with emphasis on the general rule thus illustrated. The Carthaginians have already been shown to lose the *eunoia* of their subjects in Spain. It may be added that, as early as Book I, they are in danger because they have equally lost the *eunoia* of their subjects in Africa. Polybius notices that they had treated them in a hard manner (72: πικρῶς); therefore (τοιγαροῦν) a simple messenger was all they needed to burst into passionate revolt. Once more Polybius is careful to underline the general lesson though, as all his general lessons, it does not sound very original or illuminating—people, he says proudly, should always think of the future! Indeed, the lesson has its counterpart and the demonstration is thus complete, for the Carthaginians, being then in danger and difficulty, pass the direction of the war onto Hamilcar. Hamilcar wins some success and, after his victory, he is most tolerant. He takes into his own army all those who want to join it and the others are freed (78). Now the leaders of the revolt are worried at this *philanthropia* of Hamilcar (79. 8) and they fear that the people will abandon the war they are engaged in. They find a pretext for denouncing this *philanthropia* as a crafty deceit, and they succeed in deceiving their audience. But the whole episode is obviously a demonstration showing how profitable *philanthropia* really is and how unprofitable cruelty turns out to be.[13]

The knowledge of this all-important rule motivates the great heroes on the Roman side, and most of all Scipio Africanus. For Scipio's first appearance in Polybius's history, we see him victorious in Spain; Polybius devotes several chapters to his kindness and generosity toward prisoners of all kinds; with such an attitude Scipio inspires them with a great *eunoia* and trust (x. 17. 15: εὔνοιαν καὶ πίστιν). As for hostages, they will all be safe as long as their families join the Roman alliance. Now, among the prisoners so kindly treated was the sister-in-law and daughters of King Indibilis. The king's daughters had in fact been badly treated by the Carthaginians, so that the contrast is more striking to all, but particularly to him. He comes to meet Scipio, admits that the Roman captain has been trustworthy, and joins him (x. 38. 3). He is

then promised all sorts of kind treatment from the Romans
(4: ἀπάντων τῶν φιλανθρώπων). Obviously, generosity produces help and power.

Later, the same Scipio is shown to behave in a similar
way toward the Carthaginians themselves, at the end of the
second Punic War. He is indeed ready to treat them with
more humanity than they deserve (xv. 17. 4: πρᾴως καὶ μεγα-
λοψύχως), and he offers them good and kind treatment
(7: τὰ φιλάνθρωπα τὰ διδόμενα). Hannibal is so overwhelmed
by this attitude that he is indignant at the idea that one
could refuse those unexpectedly kind terms (19. 5: τοιούτων
φιλανθρώπων). Thus is peace finally achieved. Generosity has
brought out willing submission.

Later again, Scipio uses the same policy with Prusias. This
king was ready to join Antiochos, but he received a letter sent
by Scipio and his brother explaining that the Romans didn't
overthrow any of the reigning kings but only added to their
power. As examples, the two brothers mentioned Indibilis and
Colichas in Spain, Massinissa in Africa, Pleuratos in Illyria,
Philip and Nabis in Greece; therefore, they invited Prusias to
join the Romans as these kings had done before him. Changing
his mind according to that letter, Prusias accepted the offer
(xxi. 11). Generosity once more secures friendship and alliance, that is to say, ultimately power.

It could also be added that Scipio's uncle had long ago
started such a policy in Spain, where he had besieged a number
of cities, but treated with kindness whoever received him spon-
taneously (iii. 76. 2: ἐφιλανθρώπει), taking great care that
the people should suffer no harm.

This is indeed the same policy of *eunoia* which Isocrates
had praised, with the same actual efficacy. Only the moment
and manner are slightly different. Whereas Isocrates considered the power he was speaking of as already obtained more
or less by agreement and confederacy, Polybius deals with
wars and considers the successive and isolated transformation
of enemies into allies. Hence, we have two consequences. First,
whereas Isocrates considered the general observance of rules

abiding for all, Polybius deals with particular and even personal arrangements and settlements. As soon as one gets to the Romans, one finds practical opportunism replacing the great principles of which the Greeks were so fond (even when not acting accordingly).[14] But the second and more important consequence, and difference, has nothing to do with the settlement itself but with its aim and conditions. Isocrates wished the Greeks to be rallied by the attraction of a glorious and generous action; the positive side of the policy of *eunoia* was that one should become a benefactor not of each particular state, but of Greece as a whole, and of the Greek ideal. On the other hand, Polybius describes a more realistic policy, in which the Romans try to win people over by offering them kind treatment, the assurance of suffering no harm, and generous treatment, that is to say the ability to partake in their own power.

Yet, in spite of these differences, it is obvious that Polybius was doing his best in his work to defend and praise the same doctrine that Isocrates had defended and praised in his.

In fact, this was to remain a classical theme of Roman literature. Livy formulated it, saying that no other state applied to its enemies lighter punishments (i. 28: "mitiores . . . poenas"); he has numerous examples of such behavior.[15] Sallust insists on the clemency of the ancient Romans, who reigned, he says, "beneficiis magis quam metu" and who, being offended, preferred "ignoscere quam persequi" (9. 5). And Cicero (*De Officiis* ii. 8. 26) shows that the Romans should never have preferred "metui quam cari esse et diligi."[16]

In that case, a change toward severity would be exactly equivalent to the classical type of *hybris*, and such is precisely the change that Sallust seems to deplore when he insists in the *Catiline* on the new habits of plunder (12) and when he says that the Roman authority has changed into a cruel and unbearable empire (10. 6). Perhaps, if we had the whole of Polybius's *Histories*, we might find already some misgivings about certain acts of hard repression, such as Carthage and Corinth underwent.[17] Yet we have no such hint.

This absence of misgivings could indeed surprise us more than it does if he had praised a policy of *philanthropia* in all cases and for all people, or if he had insisted that such had always been the Roman policy. But such is not the case. The virtuous attitude of Isocrates—what I would like to call the τοιγαροῦν doctrine, as all these authors are so keen on explaining that such and such a man or state was virtuous and that "therefore" (τοιγαροῦν) he had all sorts of advantages and successes—this virtuous attitude, although clearly present in Polybius, is far from giving an adequate image of the Roman policy, which is much more lucid and subtle. Therefore, we need go a little further and look a little more closely at the difference in order to grasp what Polybius didn't emphasize so clearly, but which was, all the same, at the root of the Roman use of *philanthropia*.

The Roman use of *philanthropia*, one could say, is both less general but more efficient than in Greek reflection. Now what do I mean by these two differences? First of all, how can it be said to be less general?

For a state, or a policy, it would seem that there are only two opposite attitudes: one can govern by force and by fear, or one can be kind and reckon on the goodwill of those to whom one has been kind. That is the manner in which Machiavelli presents the problem in chapter 17 of *The Prince*; he makes a bold choice in favor of the first attitude. Drawing a contrast between Hannibal and Scipio, he shows that the former was formidable and obeyed by his troops, whereas the latter was too kind and his troops revolted against him. Therefore, Machiavelli frankly accepts the condition of the Athenian Empire, for he writes: "The prince, therefore, should not be worried at the idea of having a sad reputation of cruelty, if he wants to keep his subjects united and obedient."

Machiavelli makes a choice, which was easier to do in the case of a single man having the whole power of the state in his own hands. But what of a state dealing with other states?

The attitude of the Athenians in the fifth century B.C. had rested on such a choice, which proved fatal; the optimism of Isocrates didn't prove to be more successful. Now if we read Polybius carefully, it soon emerges that the Roman policy rested not on choice but on a combination of both attitudes. The Romans shared the Athenian view that any empire is based on strength and fear, which produces obedience; but they also shared Isocrates' view—if we may call it so—that any empire needs the support of goodwill, producing alliances and, through alliances, success.

The result is that, though Polybius virtuously insists on clemency and *eunoia*, his narration does offer a perpetual oscillation between clemency and severity, between fear and goodwill.

He speaks of Scipio's clemency and of his kind terms for peace. But Antiochos is offered such hard terms that he cannot accept them (XXI. 14). The case of the Rhodians is just the same (XXIX. 19). As for Carthage, though Polybius admits that the question has been a matter of argument,[18] it is, of course, entirely destroyed—and so is the Greek city of Corinth.

In fact, Rome's clemency is extended to those who can help her and who join her party. They help her, and she helps them—against others for whom no clemency has any point or place. This is so even with Scipio Africanus, and it explains Rome's leniency toward those kings who choose to defend Rome against those she fights (XXI. 11). This leniency is based on utility and on the need of solid allies.

This feature, which makes such a great difference with Greek theory, shows more in Roman authors than it does in Polybius. It probably becomes even clearer when seen from a distance by modern authors. Montesquieu, in his *Considérations sur les causes de la grandeur des Romains et de leur décadence*, makes quite an important point of it.

I would like to quote in French a few sentences from chapter 6 which show a keen insight in politics but bring us very far indeed from sheer *philanthropia* as we had first met it. These lines describe how the Senate:

... attachait à Rome des rois dont elle avait peu à craindre et beaucoup à espérer; et il en affaiblissait d'autres, dont elle n'avait rien à espérer et tout à craindre. On se servait des alliés pour faire la guerre à un ennemi; mais, d'abord, on détruisait les destructeurs. Philippe fut vaincu par le moyen des Étoliens, qui furent anéantis d'abord pour s'être joints à Antiochus. Antiochus fut vaincu par le secours des Rhodiens; mais, après qu'on leur eût donné des récompenses éclatantes, on les humilia pour jamais, sous prétexte qu'ils avaient demandé qu'on fît la paix avec Persée. Quand ils avaient plusieurs ennemis sur les bras, ils accordaient une trêve au plus faible, comptant pour beaucoup d'avoir différé sa ruine. . . .

It wouldn't be right to say that the truth lies somewhere between Polybius's laudable insistence on *eunoia* and this Machiavellian policy of continued conquest. The truth is that both were combined, *philanthropia* being used by the side of strength, and *eunoia* being produced by the side of fear.

This transformation in the use of kindness and in the pursuit of *eunoia* makes them a less utopian means of action. But it leaves us also with less an ideal and, it would seem, with less basis for *homonoia* or concord. If Rome chooses one style or another according to her private interest of the moment, it appears that the allies should also join her or leave her according to the advantage and opportunity of their actual situation. Yet Roman greatness rose regularly and wasn't threatened with decline and fall for many centuries. I think our last task should be to try to see why—even if Polybius hasn't insisted on the idea.

The fact is that, if clemency or *philanthropia* is thus of limited and calculated scope in Roman policy, it is, when used, used without restriction. By that, I mean that a people, once accepted into alliance, is always more or less assimilated to the Romans themselves.

This was something which the Greeks were very reluctant to do. Grouping people into a new political unit could be done: it had been done at the dawn of cities. Theseus is praised for having united the Athenians into a city-state (*sunoikismos*).

However, grouping cities together was a very different matter. *Sumpoliteia*, which meant sharing the same political life with another city, could also be done, but the process seems to have taken place only in the fourth century B.C. and only between small cities. It couldn't even be thought of for great and powerful states.

Thus do we discover that the Greeks, who had, from the very beginning, a keen perception of their actual unity and consanguinity, never succeeded in giving it any political reality, whereas the very small city of Rome turned almost the whole population of the Mediterranean world into Romans.

Now, although neither Polybius nor Livy insisted on the idea, it is quite obvious that this progressive assimilation was the way in which, since the very beginning, Rome grew and rose to dominion. She gave citizenship to the people of Alba (Livy i. 28), enlisted Latin people (i. 52), admitted some Etruscans within the city (ii. 14), gave citizenship to the Sabines (ii. 22). Then, she gave citizenship to the Latins and, progressively, by organizing provinces and granting citizenship either to isolated persons, who had been devoted and true to Rome, or to whole cities and provinces, she enlarged and broadened her own political existence.

Even in this it must be acknowledged, the Romans didn't act in a simple and uniform manner. They granted various forms of rights and advantages. Montesquieu, who insists on this variety in the same chapter just quoted, says: "Ils avaient plusieurs sortes d'alliés. Les uns leur étaient unis par des privilèges et une participation de leur grandeur, comme les Latins et les Herniques; d'autres, par l'établissement même, comme leurs colonies; quelques uns par les bienfaits, comme furent Massinissa, Eumène et Attale, qui tenaient d'eux leur royaume ou leur agrandissement." It could be added that even citizenship had its various degrees: the distinction between "Latin rights" and "Roman rights" is well known.[19] The result is, of course, that the Romans could choose between the different cases and people through their ability to repay good service, thus stimulating goodwill. But the movement was always in the same direction. The same evolution brought them to create, first, a powerful city, then a powerful country, and ultimately one of the most powerful empires that ever existed. *Homonoia* ("concord") was indeed created, not without inner struggle and wars, but in a solid fashion: it was not produced by the ideal glamour of common enterprises, as Isocrates had wished in a rather optimistic way, but was produced by a deliberate extension of citizenship.

Some centuries later, people from Thrace or Spain, not to speak of the whole Byzantine Empire, were called "Romans." No Greek city could have admitted such a course. Perhaps that is why no Greek author seemed able to understand the principle and originality of such an attitude.

We only find it explained and advocated in Roman politics, and then rather late. It emerges here and there, but the main text is, of course, Claudius's speech as we have it in Tacitus (*Annals* xi. 24 ff.) and in the Table of Lyon.

Undoubtedly, the idea was not a new one.[20] The facts show it; so do one or two speeches which pave the way for Claudius's speech. One of them is known by a Greek source, the king of Alba's speech in Dionysos of Halicarnassus iii. 29, where he says that there can be no solid friendship if one doesn't share one and the same fatherland and if all are not citizens of the same state. Another one is already Latin, Canuleius's speech in Livy iv. 3–5, where he speaks in favor of extending the right of *conubium* ("marriage with citizens") and recalls that it was a tradition for Rome to receive people not only *in civitatem*, but *in patriciorum numerum*. But Claudius's speech, both in Tacitus and in the Table of Lyon, goes beyond saying that it will be good and useful to grant senatorial rank to some of the Gauls; he describes the Roman state's progressive development as due to its continually granting to other nations citizenship and political responsibility. He shows what help Rome received from these people, now completely fused with the other Romans.[21] As if to prove that this policy was indeed an answer to the problem raised by Thucydides and Isocrates, Tacitus has him insist on the contrast with

Sparta and Athens :[22] "What else," asks the emperor, "caused the ruin of Sparta and Athens, but the fact that they dealt with defeated people as with foreigners?"

Through this course, indeed, the empire ceased to be imprisoned in the initial condition Thucydides had described. It was not an empire over others, but thanks to others, and shared with those who could help. The rise of colonial elites, so brilliantly studied by Sir Ronald Syme, was the ultimate success of that policy, combining the advantages of force and leniency.

This way of organizing power, which was to prove so successful, is indeed the great invention and solution of our problem. It can be summed up under a very modern word: integration. Now, it might seem more than a little surprising that the authors—and first of all, Polybius, whom we were dealing with—didn't formulate it more clearly or more frequently. I have not included here one single quotation of Polybius. As I have already said, it might be that the idea was too distant from his Greek habits of thought and that it would have required quite an amount of reflection to grasp the difference and its importance. One could also argue that the idea appears in the very structure of his work. The *sumploke* ("intertwining structure" of the *Histories*), which shows us the Senate of Rome receiving the embassies, deciding on peace and war, and becoming progressively the Senate of the empire, is indeed the image of the *sumploke* or combination of people, which Rome established in the Mediterranean world by a shrewd but generous extension of the different rights she could bestow on people.

Now, I would like to add but one slight rectification. I have quoted twice Montesquieu's book on Rome. We shouldn't forget that this book deals with the Romans' rise and fall! The fact is that Rome had built and organized such a solid power that its ultimate fall was to remain for centuries the most fascinating problem and theme of political reflection, beginning with Gibbon, who was a great admirer of Montesquieu. How, indeed, did such an empire tumble down?

Many reasons can be alleged—even the influence of religion, if we follow Gibbon. But, if we want to keep to our theme and to the way in which the problem had been considered in Greece, I think we may select two main reasons which have pride of place and offer an answer to that problem.

One is the reason so strongly stigmatized by all Greek authors, namely, the loss of moral virtues. Gibbon and Montesquieu both mentioned it, and they were neither the first authors to do so nor the last.[23] The other reason is a result of the Roman method of organizing power. The empire grew too big. It didn't stir Rome to *hybris*, as the Greeks would have expected; perhaps it corrupted her: no doubt the inner spirit of the Romans was affected, as Roman authors saw, by the natural decay which accompanies all greatness; but that was not all: the result was also that authentic concord was finally ruined by the very means by which it had been created.[24] As the empire grew larger and larger, the Romans grew more irresponsible. The Roman army, into which too many foreign people had been admitted, became uncivilized and lost its former qualities.[25] At a late epoch, Gothic warriors, who were too numerous and too different to be relied upon, were even admitted within the very walls which ought to have protected the Roman Empire against them. The center and capital of the Roman Empire had been transferred a long distance away with the result that this Roman Empire did not depend on Rome any more. Rome had risen to power and had organized a solid power because she had been wise enough to admit other people to share her political life and dominion. But she fell partly because she had admitted too many. Even in the wise calculation of political alliances, even in the open policy of unification, *hybris* finally reappears—the old excess which the Greeks so acutely perceived the dangers of, but which they had not yet come to know in all its possible and different aspects.

My theme in this study was ambitious, and the range of authors to be considered was wide. It may seem foolish to have gone even further and cast a final glance at Latin authors as well, not to speak of their modern progeny. If only the Roman solution had proved to be the utmost and perfect procedure for attaining lasting power, that would be an excuse. But it did not prove to be so: not quite. Yet, I think this brief intrusion into Roman politics is not wholly out of place because it can help us to see more clearly the contrast between Rome and Greece. Greek ideas on the rise and fall of states were doctrines—sharp, lucid, general doctrines. As soon as we reach the Roman world, we are confronted with facts more than with doctrines. The doctrines are implicit, or they are put forward occasionally, when it helps in fostering some practical design; some room is always left for opportunity. Tracing the history of such ideas becomes more dangerous and may be tricky.

This contrast is, actually, the main justification of my whole theme. In Greece, it is possible to study the ideas of different authors about such themes as the rise and fall of states. These ideas exist, firmly formulated. What is more, they follow on one another in a sort of regular progress. Some authors try to explain, others wish to advise. Each one starts where the other had left off. This makes for a coherent discourse —so coherent that the continuity is not broken, even though so many authors are, in fact, missing.

Why is that so? It is not because of any direct influence of one author on the following one. Isocrates seems to have read Thucydides but I say "seems to," for nothing is sure. I doubt very much whether Polybius had ever read Isocrates or had even studied his Thucydides properly. The continuity is not literary. It arises from the very progress of contemporary experience and from the passion the Greeks always had for transposing this contemporary experience into general ideas. This they did in the light of the intellectual habits prevailing at that time; such a circumstance adds, of course, to the continuity. But all of them did it at all times; that was the most remarkable feature of the Greek mind. The events which in-

spired them, or which they hoped to redress, are in themselves
of no interest to us, but the doctrines remain, clear and bright.
There is no author in the modern world who isn't more or less
indebted to them, no personal reflection that can ignore them.
This, I think, had to be said, and I wish it could have been
said better for the sake of classical studies and for the love of
Greek. To me it is a cause of perpetual wonder and gratitude.

Notes

Chapter I.

1. These two facts are universally acknowledged. See J. P. Vernant, *Mythe et pensée chez les Grecs* (Paris: Maspero, 1965), pp. 22–23, who offers an interesting interpretation of this combined structure.

2. This pessimistic view seems to recur in people like Theophrastus and Dicaearchus. The latter may have shown in his *Bios Hellados* a succession of ways of life, growing worse and worse (see particularly fragment 48, Wehrli).

3. See my paper, "Thucydide et l'idée de progrès," *Annali della Scuola Norm. Sup. di Pisa* (1966): 143–91, and, more recently, E. R. Dodds, *The Ancient Concept of Progress* (Oxford: Clarendon Press, 1973), pp. 1–25.

4. In a way, it could be argued that Marxism, which posits that history will produce the victory of one class of men and a society without anything outside itself, joins the old notion of practical unification with the more modern idea of the spiritual accession of man.

5. This doesn't mean, needless to say, that, although each state rises and falls, there isn't something that keeps progressing in mankind. But, in the absence of any precise formula stating such an idea, it is only fair to say that the insistence on the idea of frailty rings a different note altogether.

6. VII. 75. 6–7, in Hobbes's translation.

7. Pol. XXIX. 21. 4.

8. *Considérations sur les causes de la grandeur des Romains et de leur décadence,* chap. 15. The paragraph begins in a way that is worthy of Greek tragedy: "C'est ici qu'il faut se donner le spectacle des choses humaines. . . ."

9. *Trach.* 131 sqq, Jebb's translation.

10. See A. Momigliano, "Time in Ancient Historiography," and C. Starr, "Historical and Philosophical Time," both in *History and Theory* 5, Beiheft 6 (1966). See also P. Vidal-Naquet, "Temps des dieux et temps des hommes," *Rev. hist. des religions* 157 (1960): 55–80.

11. See Vernant, *Mythe et pensée chez les Grecs*, p. 26: "Le cycle des âges, alors, serait bouclé et le temps n'aurait plus qu'à retourner en sens inverse."

12. See Dodds, *The Ancient Concept of Progress*, pp. 3–4, where he says that the line "seems to betray the fact that the oriental myth was cyclic," and adds: "The cyclic interpretation was not, however, what interested Hesiod."

13. Vernant, *Mythe et pensée chez les Grecs*, p. 27.

14. .Several authors have been proposed as sources for Polybius or as representing the same trend of thought; these include Panaetius, Hippodamus, Ocellus Lucanus, Critolaus, Theophrastus, Dicaearchus (see the bibliography in F. Walbank, *A Historical Commentary on Polybius* [Oxford: Clarendon Press, 1957]). All this is too uncertain to be of any use here.

15. On this discussion, see mainly: W. Theiler, "Schichten im 6 Buch des Pol.," *Hermes* 81 (1953): 296 ff.; T. Cole, "The Sources and Composition of Pol. VI," *Historia* 13 (1964): 440–86; Petzold, *Studien zur Methode des Pol. und zu ihrer hist. Auswertung*, Vestigia IX (Munich: Beck, 1969); T. Gelzer, "Ueber die Arbeitsweise des Pol.," *Sitzb. Ak. Heidelberg* (Winter, 1956). For a more balanced view, see: K. von Fritz, *The Theory of the Mixed Constitution in Antiquity* (New York: Columbia University Press, 1954); F. Walbank, *A Historical Commentary on Polybius*; K. F. Eisen, *Polybiosinterpretazionen* (Heidelberg: Winter, 1966).

16. C. O. Brink and F. Walbank, "The Construction of the Sixth Book of Polybius," *Class. Quart.* NS 4 (1954): 97.

17. For other examples of this meaning of the cycle metaphor, see my paper about cycles and circles in Greek authors, in *Le Monde Grec, Hommages à Claire Préaux* (Brussels, 1975), pp. 140–52. On the pattern of history in Herodotus, see H. R. Immerwahr, *Form and Thought in Herodotus*, Philol. Monographs 23 (Cleveland, 1966), specifically pp. 152–54.

18. Cf., among others, § 1046.

19. The title of Dicaearchus's work (see note 2) might here be misleading: he probably didn't follow such a pattern. (About Jason and the work he gave under the same title, difficulties are even greater: see *R.E.* IX. 780.)

20. τρίψεσθαί τε αὐτὴν περὶ αὐτήν; the following sentence uses the verb ἐγγηράσεσθαι, but the subject of this verb is τὴν ἐπιστήμην.

21. For other instances of the biological pattern in Book VI, see 4 (11–13), 9, and 57. On the problem of combining this view of a biological pattern, having its *akme*, with the general cycle, see the bibliography in Walbank's *A Historical Commentary on Polybius*, but mainly, Zuncan, *Rend. Ist. Lomb.* (1936): 508, and Ryffel, Μεταβολὴ πολιτειῶν (Bern, 1949), pp. 216 ff.

22. See Bodo Gatz, *Weltalter, goldene Zeit und Sinnverwandte Vorstellungen*, Spudasmata: Bd. 16 (Hildesheim: G. Olms, 1967), pp. 108–13, and R. Haüssler, "Von Ursprung und Wandel des Lebensaltervergleichs," *Hermes* 92 (1964): 313–41 (specifically pp. 319–23).

23. See, among others, the two studies mentioned in note 22.

24. I leave out the interesting but less forceful use made of the pattern by Augustine, Prudentius, and other Christian writers, for which references may be found in Haüssler's article, "Von Ursprung und Wandel des Lebensaltervergleichs."

25. See, for instance, I. 35. 9.

26. These lessons may be rather poor: see my paper, "L'utilité de l'histoire selon Thucydide," *Histoire et Historiens dans l'antiquité, Fondation Hardt* IV (1958): 41–66 (specifically p. 64).

27. *Republic*, 562b.

28. The references are: I. 82. 6; I. 124. 1; I. 144. 3; II. 64. 6; III. 10. 1; III. 82. 2.

Chapter II.

1. VI. 24. 3.

2. See, for instance, the description of what the Persians left behind them at Plataea (IX. 80). There is also a long analysis about collecting tributes in III. 89 ff.

3. Cf. *Persians* 3, 9, 45, 52, 159, 250, 751, 754.

4. The idea is given great importance in the very last chapter of Herodotus's work, when Cyrus tells his people that a richer land would spoil their valiance and therefore their power.

5. This is the only element producing power which my list has in common with that of Professor A. G. Woodhead in *Thucydides and the Nature of Power* (Cambridge: Harvard University Press, 1970). The analysis given in his book, while attempting to show how modern Thucydides can be, doesn't lay the emphasis on the notions which Thucydides, inspired by the discoveries of his own time, emphasized in his work.

6. To this reserve fund should be added the gold and silver of religious ex-votos (II. 13. 4), which could be borrowed by the state. Some of it was perhaps borrowed in the last period of the war.

7. Athens's ships, although numerous, also proved useless in the harbor of Syracuse. However, when it was thought that Athens would collapse, she didn't; her immediate reaction was to ready a new fleet (VIII. 1. 3, cf. II. 65. 12).

8. This could be true of Isocrates, in whose time Athens was poor (see A. Fuks, "Isokrates and the Social-economic Situation in Greece," *Ancient Society* (1972): 17–44 (specifically p. 31).

9. The theme recurs occasionally, and a proverb used to say that money is the best of allies for war (see Diodorus XXIX. 6, dealing with the Carthaginian victories over Rome).

10. See III. 122; VI. 7–9, but mainly V. 23; V. 36; VII. 139. Herodotus, however, has no systematic idea about it. In I. 27, Croesus is led to abandon naval equipment by the idea that each has his proper field and speciality. I would not quite agree, therefore, with A. Momigliano when he writes, "Thalassocracy, as is well-known, becomes a clear-cut idea in Herodotus," in "Sea-Power in Greek Thought," *Class. Rev.* 58 (1944), reprinted in *Secondo contributo alla storia degli studi classici* (Rome: Edizioni di storia e letteratura, 1960), pp. 57–67 (specifically p. 57).

11. See *On the Peace* 74, 77 (where the words are forcefully separated: ἡ δύναμις . . . αὕτη), 95, 101 (where there is a

vigorous pun, ἡ ἀρχή τῆς θαλάττης becoming the ἀρχή τῶν συμφορῶν), and 102 (where ταύτης before τῆς ἀρχῆς, should, I think, be kept, in spite of its omission in some of the manuscripts and in one papyrus).

12. This very corruption is shown as bringing wealth, if not power, in 705b. The same condemnation recurs in Cicero, *De Rep.* II. 3–4.

13. Diodorus XXXII. 6. 3. Cf. Appian, *Lib.* 86–89, and see Momigliano, "Sea-Power in Greek Thought," p. 66.

14. In Xenophon, Jason aims at sea power and counts on ships and money (*Hell.* VI. 1. 10); but this is only a belated dream that doesn't take form in reality.

15. See also his interest in Archimedes' inventions (VIII. 6).

16. See *Discours sur l'Histoire universelle*, part 3, chap. 6; *Considérations sur les causes de la grandeur des Romains et de leur décadence*, chap. 5. The same trend was to be continued as new instruments of war were invented: see Gibbon's insistence on the importance of the so-called Greek fire in Byzantine times.

17. This idea of training has great importance in Thucydides; his Athenians have *empeiria* on sea, his Lacadaemonians on land (II. 89. 3, for instance). Polybius also insists on the importance of training (II. 18). This means that war is useful, not only for immediate success, but for future power.

18. See also v. 66: "Athens, who was already powerful before that, became more powerful when she was rid of tyrants." One finds the reverse argument in regard to the Persians in III. 82. 5, but the passage is less general and, although it provides the conclusion, it belongs to an *antilogia* (see note 23).

19. W. H. S. Jones's translation, in the Loeb collection.

20. A. G. Woodhead, *Thucydides and the Nature of Power* (Cambridge: Harvard University Press, 1970).

21. This link is strongly emphasized by the Pseudo-Xenophon (I. 2). It is a classical theme (see Aristotle, *Politics* v. 1304a).

22. *On the Crown* 235–36. See also *Ol.* I. 4.

23. That is what Herodotus had already noticed: v. 97.

24. On this theme, see Ryffel, Μεταβολὴ πολιτειῶν, pp. 5, 84.

25. Needless to say, the same rules can be verified in other cases. For instance, the Spartan *politeia* was well calculated

for the control of each citizen though not well enough for the control of the city itself in its relations with its neighbors (see note 31).

26. This theory was prepared by the remarks on the mixed constitution of Sparta in Plato *Laws* iii. 691d–692c, and Aristotle *Pol.* 1294b.

27. On the other hand, the Carthaginian *politeia* was not mixed enough—it gave too much to the people. That is why the policy of the city was less calculated and less wise (vi. 51).

28. The praise of the mixed constitution recurs in Cicero, *De Rep.* i. 45; ii. 23; ii. 32. See also Montesquieu, *Considérations sur les causes de la grandeur des Romains et de leur décadence*, chap. 4: "Rome fut sauvée par la force de son institution."

29. *Roman Ant.* i. 5. He speaks of laws, but see the insistence on *virtuous* laws in, for instance, ii. 18–19 or ii. 63.

30. See his insistence on ἔθισμοι or ἔθη καὶ νόμιμα in i. 13. 2; vi. 56, 1; xviii. 35. 1.

31. Yet she had a good constitution for acquiring military superiority (vi. 48, cf. Aristotle *Pol.* 1324b. 7).

32. F. Walbank (*A Historical Commentary on Polybius* [Oxford: Clarendon Press, 1957] *ad* vi. 18. 5) quotes, for instance, xxxi. 25. 3 ff. as an example of corruption, but it is not yet one that could endanger the state.

Chapter III.

1. On this difference between Herodotus and Aeschylus, see the quotations collected in my article, "La vengeance comme explication historique dans l'œuvre d'Hérodote," *Revue des Études grecques* 84 (1971): 316, n. 1.

2. This fault was the murder of a king; though Herodotus doesn't mention it here, another murder of another king also leads to the same punishment (i. 13) — Herodotus's very hesitation, disproved by this double explanation, shows the unsteadiness of his reflection in that field.

3. See, for instance, vi. 91, also iii. 126, and viii. 106, with the reservations formulated in p. 317 of my article quoted above in note 1.

4. For Cambyses, there is no pattern at all. He is overconfident, according to Herodotus (who, in that case, probably exaggerates), but he is overconfident because he is mad; his madness is not a punishment of overconfidence (III. 25).

5. He also offended the dead: see, e.g. VII. 238. 3.

6. In regard to the rise of the Persian Empire, it would only be fair to say that there is a good explanation, both psychological and political, showing that any conquest leads to further conquests, either through a sort of challenge or for reasons of security; see Atossa in III. 133, and Xerxes himself in VII. 8.

7. It could be added that the word "hybris" is generally used for the arrogance or mischief of individuals, without much religious implication. In III. 48. 1, the ὕβρισμα of Samos toward Corinth is indeed a most pious behavior with regard both to gods and general morality.

8. About the advice "not to be a prey" to such feeling or fate (μὴ παθεῖν), see the examples collected in my *Thucydide et l'impérialisme athénien* (Paris: Les Belles Lettres, 1947), pp. 270–74 (English translation, Oxford: Blackwell, 1963).

9. 741 ff.:

> Ὁ δ'αὖ τότ' εὐτυχής,
> λαβὼν πένης ὡς ἀρτίπλουτα χρήματα,
> ὕβριζ', ὑβρίζων τ' αὖθις ἀνταπώλετο.

As for Thucydides, see III. 39. 4; IV. 17. 4; 65. 4; VI. 11. 5; also, though not in a speech, V. 14. 1.

10. See G. E. M. de Ste Croix, "The Character of the Athenian Empire" *Historia* 3 (1954): 1 ff. I have discussed that view (after some others) in "Thucydides and the Cities of the Athenian Empire," *Bulletin of the Institute of Classical Studies* (University of London) 13 (1966): 1–12.

11. The word ἐνάγειν is used for the people's irrational wish in II. 21. 3, for the Locrians' irrational appeal in IV. 24. 1, and for the Corinthian and Syracusan wish to extend war in VII. 18. 1 (cf. VIII. 78). The same word is used for Cleon's policy of continued war in IV. 21. 3, and for Alcibiades' egoistical tendency for conquest in VI. 15. 2.

12. The ὁρμαῖς here alluded to have to do with internal policy as much as with foreign policy. This aspect of *hybris* will

be dealt with in the last part of this chapter. On this passage and its meaning, see M. Gelzer, "Nasica's Widerspruch gegen die Zerstörung Karthagos," *Phil.* 86 (1931): 271 ff.

13. The following part of the sentence confirms what we have said of the meaning of flattery, for it adds: "you consider future actions, from what is artfully presented to you, as possible to realize."

14. Whatever the meaning one gives to ἀρχή here, it is obviously not the state's power.

15. About the progress of personal ambition during the Peloponnesian War, see my paper, "Les Phéniciennes d'Euripide et l'actualité dans la tragédie grecque," *Rev. Phil.* 39 (1965): 28–47.

16. See later, p. 60.

17. See my two papers, "Vocabulaire et propagande, ou les premiers emplois du mot ὁμόνοια, " *Mélanges P. Chantraine* (1972): 199–209, and "Les différents aspects de la concorde dans l'œuvre de Platon," *Rev. Phil.* 46 (1972): 7–20.

18. This goes on in Gibbon. See, for instance, chapter 52 about the divisions among the Arabs after their conquest. As for Montesquieu, he shows, in the following chapter, how the very size of the empire may have a corrupting influence: the armies and their leaders lose contact with the government and, thereby, lose their obedience. This danger had already been observed by the Greeks in the case of the Spartan kings; it was not without influence on the Spartan policy and its rejection of imperialism.

19. See A. G. Woodhead, *Thucydides and the Nature of Power* (Cambridge: Harvard University Press, 1970), chap. 1.

20. They don't say "worthy of dominion," but "worthy of not being so much exposed to jealous criticism as regards our dominion." There is a slight difference; still, this notion of being "worthy" echoes the Funeral Speech.

21. Sparta does it also; the words *ôphelimon* and *xumpheronta* are applied to her with insistence in I. 75. 5, and 76. 2.

22. See the word *xumpheron* in VI. 83. 2 (twice) and 87. 3; *ôphelia* is equally insisted upon.

23. See, for Torone, V. 3. 4; for Skione, V. 32. 1; for Melos, V. 116. 4.

24. On this evolution, see F. Wehrli, "Zur politischen Theorie der Griechen: Gewaltherrshaft und Hegemonie," *Mus. Helv.* (1968): 215–25.

25. He would like, of course, to have the rise and to avoid the causes leading to downfall: his plan for that is discussed in chapter 4.

26. Demosthenes also complains that the crisis of the city has deprived the citizens of their courage and readiness to fight personally for her sake. This is a new theme, and a new danger, that had not yet appeared during the Peloponnesian War, but that was to recur in the case of Rome.

27. See *Catiline* 3, 10, 36–38; *Jugurtha* 1, 4, 8 etc. . . . This moral trend is important, as Sallust's theme may be summed up as a study of the decline and fall of the Republic even by such a nonmoralizing author as Sir Ronald Syme.

28. *Considérations sur les causes de la grandeur des Romains et de leur décadence,* chap. 10.

29. Consider the revealing title of a modern book by C. Ritter, *The Corrupting Influence of Power.*

30. See Thucydides i. 18. 3; Polybius i. 63–64.

31. It started in Aristoteles (*Pol.* vii. 1334ab); see also Xenophon *Cyrop.* iii. 1. 26. It occurs without being insisted upon in Polybius (see xxxii. 13. 16); but it has pride of place in Sallust (perhaps taking after Poseidonius).

Chapter IV.

1. This is true of other cities, not of the condition within the city, where one part of the population was under strict rule and was always ready to revolt. Such a situation weighed terribly on the fate of Sparta; this explains both her unwillingness to take part in distant enterprises and her vulnerability to anything that threatened the social order (Pylos being a clear example of such vulnerability).

2. v. 4. 1. About the scandal in Greece, see vi. 3. 11; Isocrates *Paneg.* 126; and *Peace* 98.

3. The other reason was that all conditions were different for Athens (such as geographical conditions, social conditions, military organization, and so on).

4. It may also have been a result, not of actual excess (which is the old *hybris* pattern), but of lack of strength.

5. Cf. "*Eunoia* in Isocrates, or the Political Importance of Creating Good Will," *J.H.S.* 78 (1958): 92–101, where I also borrow the main idea there dealt with.

6. See, particularly, 28, 29–30, 32, 100, 105, 140.

7. See Herodotus ix. 27. 6; for Thucydides: i. 75. 1; 76. 2; ii. 41. 3; vi. 83. 1.

8. On the other hand, Montesquieu, *Considérations sur les causes de la grandeur des Romains et de leur décadence*, chap. 9, suggests that different laws are appropriate to the acquisition or preservation of power.

9. The Greek words are, significantly enough, φθόνος, ὀργή, and μῖσος.

10. See also the glory of Antigonos for having spared Sparta and treated Greece so well (v. 9. 10); but Polybius, there, speaks of glory, not of political advantage.

11. Demosthenes (*On the Crown*, 231) speaks of a "pretended" *philanthropia*, which he explains by the firm resistance of Athens.

12. Again, the idea is stressed by a general formulation: Scopas did not know that desire . . . (οὐκ εἰδὼς ὅτι . . .), and this did show in his case with exceptional clarity (ἐμφανέστατον δὲ συνέβη γενέσθαι περὶ τὸν ἄνδρα τοῦτον). For other examples of the same idea, see xv. 21. 2; 24. 4; xxiii. 15.

13. In the same episode, we also find the advantages of being moderate even when a city is a small one. Two of the cities that had revolted against the Carthaginians cannot come to terms because they know that their behavior was such as to make mercy impossible, which shows, says Polybius, of what great consequence moderation can be (88. 3). This feeling is what Diodotus had described in Thucydides, but, as befitted the theme of his speech, he only drew the lesson with regard to the domineering state.

14. When he deals with the Greeks, Polybius is happy to show *eunoia* created by virtue. Such is the case of the Achaean League, whose virtue, freedom, and habits of equality won the Peloponnese by sheer goodwill, which resulted in the success and political importance of this league (ii. 38, 42).

15. See, for instance, i. 52 and ii. 22, about the Latins, who are grateful for such treatment ("liberaliter habiti cultique in calamitate sua").
16. On this tradition, see M. Gelzer, *Von Römischen Staat* 1 (1943): 47.
17. See the remarks of A. Momigliano at the Budé Congress of Rome (April, 1973) published in the *Actes du Congrès* (Paris: Les Belles-Lettres, 1975): 184–94.
18. This is confirmed by the previous discussion we find in Plutarch, between Cato and Scipio Nasica (*Cato* 27. 2–5; see chap. 3, note 12 of this study).
19. On this question, see A. N. Sherwin-White, *The Roman Citizenship* (Oxford: Clarendon Press, 1939).
20. This is emphatically repeated both in J. Carcopino, *Les étapes de l'impérialisme romain* (Paris: Hachette, 1961), p. 206, and in P. Fabia "A propos de la Table Claudienne," *R.E.A.* 33 (1931): 259–60. In a way, it is obvious. But nowhere do we find in Latin such a firm description of the doctrine, which is generally referred to only by allusion.
21. On other aspects of Claudius's policy of unification, see A. Momigliano, *Claudius, the Emperor, and his Achievement* (Cambridge: Heffer and Sons, 1934), pp. 60 ff. Caesar's policy could also afford interesting proofs.
22. The idea is not in the Table; Carcopino thinks it was not in the speech, but Fabia believes it probably was ("A propos de la Table Claudienne," p. 240). The problem has no bearing on our theme.
23. See, for Gibbon, chaps. 2 and 3 and the end of chap. 7.
24. Montesquieu, *Considérations sur les causes de la grandeur des Romains et de leur décadence*, chap. 9: "Pour lors, Rome ne fut plus cette ville dont le peuple n'avait eu qu'un même esprit, un même amour pour la liberté. . . ."
25. See Gibbon, chap. 3.

Index of Passages in Ancient Authors Cited

The figures in italics refer to the pages of this book. Some references to the ancient authors are given with more detail here than in the text.